9 RULES OF ENGAGEMENT

HARPER

An Imprint of HarperCollins*Publishers*

9 RULES OF ENGAGEMENT

A Military Brat's Guide

to Life and Success

HARRIS FAULKNER

HarperCollins books may be purchased for educational, business, or sales promotional use. For information, please email the Special Markets Department at SPsales@harpercollins.com.

FIRST EDITION

Title page image courtesy of Shutterstock/pashabo

Library of Congress Cataloging-in-Publication Data has been applied for.

ISBN 978-0-06-269751-6

18 19 20 21 22   LSC   10 9 8 7 6 5 4 3 2 1

My deepest gratitude to my parents, Shirley and Bob.

You taught me everything there is to know about courage, grace, and love.

CONTENTS

PREFACE

When I was a little girl, my father, who was a high-ranking officer, pilot, and an avionics specialist in the United States military, would hoist me up onto the elevator—the flight control surface located at the tail of his airplane. From up there I could get a glimpse of the world as he saw it. Always eager for an even better view, I wanted time in the cockpit too. That required special permission, which wasn't often granted, but my dad would share his perspective with me in other ways. We'd have enlightening conversations every opportunity we could get. We'd discuss life and the military values he had learned to apply to its many challenges.

Today, as a breaking news anchor, I sometimes feel as if I'm back on the elevator of that plane, looking at the world and events as they unfold around me. I've assumed some of the role my father played, trying to convey the details, importance, and meaning of these events to my viewers. From where I sit now, I see people strained by the rapid rate of social change. Technology has made our lives both more efficient and more demanding. I see people squeezed by the shifting economies, not only by disappearing jobs, but by disappearing industries. I see people's morals and values being tested too. I also see that many have fallen out of meaningful dialogue with people of differing viewpoints.

In this climate, I find myself returning to the touchstones of my youth, realizing more clearly just how lucky I was to grow up as the daughter of a lieutenant colonel. Because the military exists to deal with challenging situations, so much of what they teach our troops about achieving success in trying times applies to us civilians trying to succeed in these times. I may not have served myself, but I grew up witnessing service, and it was perhaps my most foundational experience.

For a little background, I'm what's called a *brat* in military circles. It's an endearing term used to describe the children of officers and is actually an acronym for <u>B</u>orn <u>R</u>aised <u>A</u>nd <u>T</u>rans-ferred, which describes my early days perfectly. My mother gave birth to me at Fort McPherson in Atlanta, Georgia. A short while later we were living in Stuttgart, Germany. We relocated several more times after that to various cities and military outposts before I finally ventured to college in Santa Barbara, California. Being given the honorary rank of brat is the armed services' way of say-ing thank you to us kids for having grit too. They understand that when one member of a family joins the military, the whole family bears the weight of their service. We sacrifice time with that parent while they are deployed; we move wherever our loved one is needed; we uproot our lives; we leave our friends behind; and we start all over again with a supportive and positive attitude because it helps our loved one do his or her job effectively and return home to us safely. We are also expected to have much of the same discipline as our commissioned parent has, because we are considered a reflection of their ability to lead.

Although the connotation of the word *brat*, as it's used by the general public, isn't flattering, I think I was "spoiled" in the best of ways. I got to travel to some pretty awesome places, learn other people's customs, and see what works in their world differently than in ours. I also got to witness our troops returning from battles won and lost, and to hear some of the thinking that led to victory and some of the thinking that ultimately helped formulate better strategies from the lessons of defeat.

I'm sure it won't surprise you to learn that I kept a diary—actually, quite a number of them over the years. The budding journalist in me was always listening, observing, and documenting the experience. There was so much to take in. Just hearing about how my dad and other military personnel approached challenges when we were in the midst of war, and later learning how we maintained peace during the time when my father worked for the Joint Chiefs of Staff at the Pentagon, became the basis of my own views about success and how to attain it.

The US military is known the world over for its advanced technology as well as the prowess, skill, and dedication of its service members. When you grow up in the company of its leaders, as I did, you understand that this greatness is something that is *cultivated*. In other words, greatness is taught, and as such, we can all learn to be as accomplished in our own lives and fields of pursuit as our country's troops are.

And that really is the purpose of this book. The desire to excel is a very real part of human nature and some would argue that it is inherent in the American makeup. People in this country have always had a yearning to be great and we always will. A host of important issues in our society will continue to be hotly debated and I want to be right at the forefront covering them. Some issues may even remain undecided for a while, but in the meantime, we can at least take charge of our individual paths to success.

To do so, we can draw upon the best resources around us for guidance. In my case, that guidance lies in my diaries—all the copious notes I took over the years observing how the military repeatedly overcomes challenges and achieves its goals.

In those journals, I've kept lessons from conversations with my dad, events in my own life and in the world at large. And these lessons weren't just learned from clear-cut victory. My father and the US military have had their fair share of trials and tribulations. My dad did two tours of duty in Vietnam. That was a war where we as a nation really had to stop and reassess our approach and what winning in that context even meant. As a result of those tough times, whole pages of my journal were filled with reflections about character and purpose.

When I frequently revisited those notes as a teen and twenty-something, I picked up recurring themes. Basic tenets started to emerge. I adapted some and applied them to my life. I was amazed at the outcome. I continued to make them my own—to make them relevant to my interactions off base as well as on. The military loves mottos, so I followed their lead. Most of these tenets lent nicely to being remembered with short, pithy sayings. Soon, I realized I had crafted some really practical and helpful rules to live by. Life continued to test and refine these rules.

I'm still very connected to military friends and colleagues, but I've been living a civilian lifestyle for years now. And I can tell you, these rules, with their military underpinnings, still serve me well. They're universal. They guided me through some difficult experiences, not the least of which was my mother's passing, and a serious health crisis my father braved and fortunately rebounded from. And, of course, they've helped me plan a career path, seek increasingly more challenging and rewarding positions, win industry recognition and awards, and make choices that continue to enrich my marriage and family life.

When I realized how thirsty people were for similar guidance, I knew I had to share some of this thinking with more than just family and close friends. So I began a speaking tour, giving motivational talks to large public and private audiences. The experience was so rewarding for me and for those in attendance that I decided to compile the best of these rules in a book for even more people's benefit.

When introducing these rules, a point I often make is that sometimes it just takes being a living example of what you firmly believe in to change others' hearts and minds on a subject. If we wish for America to enjoy even greater glory than ever before, then we ourselves must strive to be the best individuals we can be. As the adage goes, "A rising tide lifts all boats." Perhaps the end to the divide that we are experiencing will come when we each strive to be our personal best.

What I believe makes this book even more useful are the additional insights offered by a variety of people who have served or have closely supported those who've served in the military. They include military spouse Paola Harrell (the widow of Major General Ernest James Harrell); Republican congresswoman and retired US Air Force Colonel Martha McSally; Democratic congresswoman and current major in the Hawaii Army National Guard Tulsi Gabbard; and the retired and much esteemed four-star general Jack Keane.

Just as the best reporting digs far beneath the headlines, the best advice comes from delving deep into the experiences that inspired it. Among the many truths I believe you'll discover in my rules, my father's stories, and these contributors' reflections is that the drive to succeed, when supported by powerful principles, has the potential to help people *attain* a better life, *protect* their quality of life, and even *save* lives.

I wrote this book as a salute to all of our troops—past, present, and future—and to their families, my own especially. I intend it as a salute to you readers as well. Many of you are also my viewers, and I suspect you picked this book up because you are looking to be the best person and citizen you can be. I hope these collective words help you achieve that goal. I sincerely wish you the success you seek and deserve.

—HARRIS FAULKNER

9 RULES OF ENGAGEMENT

INTRODUCTION: LEARNING TO TRUST IN YOUR OWN POTENTIAL

It's two o'clock in the morning. A young company commander—an officer of a combat unit supporting American troops in Vietnam—is sleeping as soundly as one can during wartime. He is stationed in Đông Hà, the northernmost town of South Vietnam, just below the DMZ. A surprise mortar attack rocks him from his bed. He is immediately jolted into fight-or-flight mode.

As the S-3 of the battalion—the staff person in charge of operations—he instinctively sprints in the direction of the command bunker where all plane arrivals and departures are controlled. The blasts hit the center of the base in quick succession and as they do, they tear up all the buildings and terrain in their wake. The officer pauses momentarily to get his bearings then darts a block and a half farther until he falls into a ravine. Shrapnel flying overhead just narrowly misses hitting him. Cries from the wounded are barely distinguishable from the piercing screams of the bombs as they're launched through the air. It looks to him as if the base is taking fire from all angles. He lifts himself up from the blood-soaked ground and takes off again, running until he reaches his destination. Pulling rifles off the wall, he turns them over to whoever has free hands. He can't even think about assessing the damage to himself until after he gets four or five teams up into the air in roughly thirty-five to forty seconds.

He had helped install this airfield just four months earlier and had hooked up all the avionics in the towers, so even in the dark of night and in the rain of fire he knows how to navigate it well. It is from here that the MACVs, USAV command helicopters, and fixed-wing aircraft take off and land daily. And just as important, it is here where they are repaired and maintained after each mission run and battle.

Only in the aftermath of the fighting, with adrenaline still coursing through his body, does this young commander realize that his leg has been badly torn up by debris from the explosives' shell casings.

As you may have guessed by now, the young officer in that real-life story is my father, Bobby Harris, and as scary as that combat experience had been, it wasn't the only harrowing situation he would find himself in during his twenty-year military career. I grew up hearing several such stories and I still shudder to think about his many close calls.

But I picked this particular story to start with—as difficult as it is to tell—because it speaks volumes about trusting in your own potential. All those who pressed on, who assumed their battle roles, and who fought that night despite the fear, confusion, and imminent threat of losing life and limb had to have exceeded their own expectations. None of them could've imagined having the strength and presence of mind to resist such a devastating attack—and yet they did.

When the military trains you, this is one of the many deadly scenarios they are preparing you for. They know from their vast experience that with the right tools, practice, and hidden reserve deep inside you that you'll rise to the occasion and defend your-self and your country.

From the moment the armed services set out to recruit young men and women, they not only project confidence in your po-tential to be this brave and mighty, they also project confidence in their ability to draw that potential out of you. Just think about the countless ad campaigns they've run over the years. If the slo-gan "We Want You" doesn't exude faith in your potential, then certainly "Be All That You Can Be," "Army of One," "Army Strong," or "Accelerate Your Life" do. These words are far more than marketing.

Anyone who has served will tell you that they can't imagine what would happen if the military didn't drive its troops, from the moment they enlisted, to believe in their own potential—or if the powers that be didn't throw every available resource be-hind those troops to validate and make that belief a reality.

Without this belief in your own abilities, both the number of lives and the number of battles lost would be staggering. To get you to trust in yourself is the very reason they put you through the rigors of boot camp. They teach you every conceivable sur-vival skill and drill you until you can practically respond to the threat in your sleep the way my father did in the previous story. They test you to prove to yourself and to them that you are ready to face the challenges ahead. They choose specialties that match your skills, and they give you further education and training to enhance those skills. Then they send you to the parts of the ser-vice that need your skills the most. If you don't emerge with a stronger sense of your own abilities then, I'm not sure what could possibly instill greater confidence in yourself.

They do all of this because the physical training is absolutely necessary to survive, but so too is your mind-set. You have to trust you will be flexible enough to apply the right skill to the right challenges.

OVERCOMING THE ODDS

Trusting in our own potential is just as vital for those of us who aren't engaged in life and death skirmishes every day as it is for warriors. We all still face challenges where we may have much to lose and we all still need confidence to overcome them. I tell you this because in the absence of hard-driving drill sergeants to ensure that we believe in, exercise, and increase our potential every day, we have to remember to do these things ourselves.

There were many opportunities for me to learn about the power of trusting in my potential when I was growing up. Both of my parents encouraged my sister Annissa and me to believe in ourselves. It wasn't necessarily a mantra, but the message came through in the way they prompted us to try new things and to stick with them as if nothing was beyond our reach. They always seemed to know how far we could stretch before we knew it. They had a good measure of our potential and we trusted in that measure until we learned to raise the bar on our own.

Throughout my childhood I also witnessed my share of nervous recruits transform into self-assured, intrepid soldiers once they had been through training and certainly after they returned from their first tour of duty. Initially the proof was in how much their running times improved or in how many more push-ups they could do, but in time it showed in the way they walked around base with increased pride. You knew they were surprising themselves with what they could do. Watching them grow and test their limits, I came to understand that we all have more potential than we think.

And believe me, every time I heard the story that opens this chapter, I thought about how capable my father was amid all that chaos and danger. The details of what transpired that night quickly became a powerful lesson in trusting your own potential because no one walks into the military on day one ready for that kind of scene. You have to practice something a million times, and get it right just as often, in order to develop both the kind of rote survival skills he exhibited and the kind of belief in your potential that we are talking about.

Of course, this was true of my dad just as it was true for every military recruit. On the surface, my father's military career appeared destined. First there's the coincidence of his birthday, June 14, 1937, which also happens to be the anniversary of the founding of the US Army. And there is also his lifelong hobby of collecting and building model airplanes, which should have foreshadowed his specialty in aviation. But if you heard stories about his struggles as a very young boy, you might not have seen this path for him as clearly.

The man who is now a retired lieutenant colonel actually grew up a poor boy in the sticks of East Texas. Although he taught himself to read before entering grade school and was a stellar student throughout, it was far from guaranteed that he would get a college education or that he would have many job opportunities beyond that. No one he knew from his school had enjoyed the kind of success he envisioned for himself. What complicated matters was that he had severely underdeveloped vocal cords—a condition that left him unable to speak until age thirteen. And if that doesn't make you doubt a future military career, consider this: When he finally became of age to enlist, America was engaged in the Vietnam War—the most unpopular and controversial conflict it had ever been in. That war also coincided with the start of the civil rights movement. As you can imagine, very few men of color were eager to fight on behalf of a country that was bleeding from the South over racism and hatred. Under these circumstances, the odds that my dad's life would go the way it did were slim, but he trusted in his own potential. What happened between age thirteen and that mortar attack is what really inspired me, and in many ways inspired all the rules to follow.

Strangely enough it was his love of basketball that set events in motion. His school was so small that their team was made up of kids from every grade. Although he possessed natural talent, he had to practice to be as good as some of the older boys. It was a real endorsement when they believed in him enough to put the ball in his hands during the last seconds of a close game. Being clutch like that was such a great feeling that he worked even harder to make sure he was always ready for those moments. In time, he and his team made it all the way to the state championships. But even before that happened, he realized that if he believed as much in his potential to talk as he did in his potential to improve his game, he might just be able to find his voice. He understood that in the same way an athlete has to work hard to develop his core, arms, and leg muscles to play well, he would have to work hard to develop his throat muscles to speak well. He did his vocal exercises as often and as long as he shot hoops after school. With patience and perseverance, the sound came. It's amazing—most people who know my dad now seem to hang on his every word when he is telling a story, and his unit back in

Vietnam certainly listened to his every command. I think they'd be very surprised to learn that talking didn't come easily to him.

To this day, my dad still believes that you can do anything if you want to badly enough *and* if you practice. There is no end to your potential if these two factors are involved. He loves to point to the example of Steph Curry, who challenges himself to make five hundred three-pointers a day, even during the off-season. You can be born with lots of innate skill, but you don't get to be the best shooter in the NBA without putting in the work. These are qualities, by the way, that my dad not only sees in the MVPs of his favorite sports teams, but also in the military's much-admired Special Forces.

Since trusting in his own potential carried him this far, my father pursued a bachelor of science degree from Prairie View A&M College in Texas and followed that with a master's in engineering from Georgia Tech. He was preparing himself to build more than just model airplanes. He interrupted his graduate work for a while, resuming it later, because the Vietnam War was under way and the civil rights movement was also picking up steam, as I mentioned earlier. Both were aggressively recruiting people to their cause.

The draft was in effect, so many young men had no choice but to head into battle. The rest were free to contest our involvement in the conflict or to march for equal rights. Protests—both peaceful and turbulent—were everyday occurrences on college campuses and elsewhere across the country. Faced with a choice as to what to do, my father opted to assert his independence differently than many others would have. He volunteered to fight in Vietnam.

Shortly before shipping off to Saigon Airfield, he had a chance meeting with a representative from the Student Nonviolent Co-ordinating Committee (SNCC)—an activist group to which such civil rights leaders as John Lewis and Julian Bond belonged. When this representative attempted to change my father's mind, he told her that he strongly believed they both served different but equally important roles in progressing black lives forward at that time. She and her supporters would need to be in every nook and cranny of the country for the battle against racism to be won, but he suspected correctly that it would take a long time—years and possibly decades—for that goal to come to fruition. In the meantime, he saw that he could attain a greater degree of personal freedom within the structure of the military. He understood that if he performed the measurable steps demanded of him, especially in light of his considerable technical skills, he could quickly climb the ranks of the Army and be freer and more successful as an in-dividual than he could ever be if he stayed behind and joined the civil rights movement. Simply put, the military needed men in great numbers. It didn't matter what their race, ethnicity, height, weight, or eye color were. If those men could fight from the sky well enough to survive the enemy's newest penchant for blowing up planes from the ground, and if they had the added skills to re-pair and maintain those fighter planes, then they'd be rock stars.

My dad recently explained his decision to me in even more eloquent terms, saying, "This is probably difficult to understand if you have not lived in the years that I lived, but the military was the first chance I had at a real freedom from home—a freedom from the pressures of having to be alert about something as simple as a drinking fountain. I don't think that I can state it any clearer than that."

When I think about the collective obstacles my dad successfully overcame in his early life, I certainly see and appreciate the power of trusting in your own potential. But it was hearing this specific story—the story of why my father joined the military—that impacted me the most, and motivated me to trust in my own potential too.

By the way, the beauty of my father's approach to securing greater freedom for himself is that it went a long way toward securing freedom for others too. When he succeeded at his goal of attaining increased independence, respect, and purpose within the military and society at large, he stood as a role model for others who wished to enjoy those same liberties. His service also reflected an understanding of what the US military hoped to accomplish through the Vietnam War. By fighting against communism, the US aimed to preserve freedoms for those who were facing severe oppression. My dad remains in awe of the ideals he fought for back then, telling me recently, "I certainly understand how this nation is outfitted to declare that it is a free country. It is because of those old guys—I don't know where they got their smarts from, but they were wise enough to write that constitution. And if you read that thing and you live to it, this is the freest nation you are ever going to see. I don't think you're ever going to come by another one like it."

Although my father was pained, confused, and conflicted when he returned from two tours of duty in Vietnam and people spat or yelled derogatory comments at him because he was a veteran or because the color of his skin was different than theirs, he always met their animosity with his trademark vision and understanding. "I would rather fight for this country as it struggles than go anywhere else," he would say. He is a true patriot and in many ways a patient teacher. He isn't afraid of conflict and often remarks that, "Political dialogue, as nasty as it is, is a privilege." He very clearly trusts in the nation's potential to overcome division, just as he did. And that is a trust I share with him.

Because of his belief in self, my dad did indeed obtain the freedom and mobility he sought as a young man. He ultimately worked at the Pentagon for the Joint Chiefs of Staff overseeing US Aviation operations all over the world. He performed many duties in that capacity. Among them, he helped maintain our presence in key regions after the war and he also conducted the safe dismantling and clearing of military power from the shores of North Africa and the Mediterranean. I'm proud of the path he took and the wisdom and experiences it provided him.

RAISING MY HOPES

I clearly ripped a page from my dad's playbook when I was preparing for my future. My passion for journalism was apparent from a young age just as his passion for airplanes was. I was driven and inquisitive too, but my secret skill is that I am an active listener. Because my father couldn't speak until he was in his teens he perfected the art of participating in conversations with his ears and I picked that skill up by his example. I really do believe in the adage "God gave us two ears and one mouth so we would listen twice as much as we talk." I also believe in training and conditioning myself to meet my goals.

For all these reasons and many more, I knew in my heart that I had the potential to rise to the top. So I dived right in. At first it may not have seemed like I had a plan, but at every step I evaluated what was going to get me to the next level and I went for it. I began my career in Los Angeles as a freelance writer before interning at a local TV station. From there, I moved to a variety of different cities garnering experience as a local reporter, a daytime news anchor, and an evening news anchor, respectively. I even squeezed live radio in at some point so I could get experience hosting a talk show, and became a correspondent for *A Current Affair* so I could get some exposure to the ins and outs of covering crime stories. But it was at the Fox News Channel where I attained one of my longest-held goals. At some point early in my exploration I set my eye on becoming a breaking-news anchor, and finally it was happening on the primetime show *Fox Report Weekend.*

Primetime.

You read that, right?

It was a huge deal. Not just for me, but for the industry. If you turned to any of the other cable networks during that peak broadcast block, there was no way that you'd find another face like mine. Even today, people of color—especially women of color—are terribly underrepresented on cable during those vital news-viewing hours. So believe me, I had to trust in my potential. A lot of people were watching and hanging their own hopes and dreams on me doing well.

For the longest time, I worked six days a week and prepared to start all over again on the seventh day. Every position I held and every broadcast I did was like a dry run for the next one. And just as my dad had his clutch moments on the basketball court, I had mine in the studio. I can't tell you how many times I've been asked to fill in on ensemble shows that are not my own—shows I'm not even likely to inherit one day. But I always caught that ball and ran with it because (1) it's good practice, (2) it's an honor to be trusted to perform well, and (3) it's a chance to prove my further potential.

If I can take the show I'm filling in on to a ratings win, then that's a triumph for the whole team.

It was this spirit and belief in the limitlessness of growth that led me to *Outnumbered*, a program I've been cohosting since it debuted on April 28, 2014, and more recently to *Outnumbered Overtime with Harris Faulkner*, the relatively new show I've been anchoring since October 2, 2017.

Together these two programs enable me to do the things I've enjoyed most in my broadcast career, all at the same time. On *Outnumbered*, I cohost with three other women and a guy in the middle whom we "outnumber." We get to examine the top news stories of the day as well as the leading political and cultural issues dominating the headlines. Then on *Outnumbered Overtime with Harris Faulkner*, which directly follows *Outnumbered* in the day-time lineup, I am able to track and more fully cover a few of the day's most important emerging news stories in real time. I can utilize the resources of Fox News Channel's journalists in the field, conduct one-on-one interviews with the latest newsmakers, and engage in deep discussions with the network's top contributors so that the coverage of breaking news is as complete as possible. It really doesn't get more fun and interesting than that.

It's humbling to see so many of my TV dreams coming true. Recently I moved to a new office. I was taking down a decorative decal I had custom made a long time ago that hung prominently on the wall across from my desk when it occurred to me that I am constantly telling myself to trust in my own potential in one way or another. The words on the decal read: "Just a girl who decided to go for it." I always liked this saying because the "Just a girl" part reminds me of where I started from and encourages me to keep humble in the face of my success, while the "who decided to go for it" reminds me to continue to strive to fulfill my potential. I smiled at the synchronicity of the message. I was having a moment of self-doubt as we are all apt to have before stepping into a new role—one I've wanted for a very long time. I had recognized that this latest development in my life was *big*, and I wondered if it might actually be *too* big. I asked myself if I really thought I had what it takes. The words on the decal reassured me that I did. I had filled big roles before and had even grown into some. Just thinking about this saying, which I had clung to for so many years, convinced me that I could do it again. It was actually telling me to trust in my own potential.

BEING YOUR OWN BEST CHAMPION

I must admit that I got a sudden jolt of motivation as I was writing the previous paragraphs. There is something about taking stock of the things you've done up until the present moment that proves your capabilities to the naysayer in your head. Making a list of the challenges you've overcome and the triumphs you've had helps you realize how much potential you've already fulfilled. It will give you the confidence to reach for that next goal.

Even looking at the times you tried and failed tells you a lot about your resilience and capacity for growth. Potential isn't only about the great qualities and aptitude we already have in store—it's also about what we add to ourselves with every experience we have and with every effort we make. So draw up that list now. You might be surprised by the confidence it gives you and the push it provides to go do something that ensures another great growth spurt.

I'd also encourage you to think about one of the primary appeals the military held for my dad: He liked the fact that there are clearly defined steps to getting promoted to each rank—to living up to the potential each stripe represents. You have to fulfill one manageable goal at a time before you can arrive at the big one. Every time you set and achieve a measurable and realistic goal you will be gaining faith in your abilities to achieve the really big one at the end of the process. It's important to aim high, but rushing in to attain that final goal before all the other pieces are in place will only make you doubt your potential. Remember, trust is something you build. So start racking up trust by doing one thing each day that furthers your goal or makes you a better you.

To help me remember to do that, I collect inspirational quotes much like the one on the decal that hung on my office wall. I've shared a few of these quotes below. Hopefully they will inspire you to take the kinds of steps that build trust in yourself as well:

Be the person you needed when you were younger.

—AYESHA SIDDIQI

You cannot give another human the responsibility of your happiness.

—TARAJI P. HENSON

I want to inspire people. I want someone to look at me and say, "Because of you, I didn't give up."

—ANONYMOUS VIRAL MEME

Rule #1

RECRUIT YOUR SPECIAL FORCES

My father once told me a story that illustrates how important it is to have a support team lined up for those moments when you really need their skills. It involves an incident that occurred just outside of Vũng Tàu. He had successfully dropped off troops, picked up supplies from a waiting ship, and was taking off again to head back to base. It was a flight pattern he was familiar with, having flown it before. He had been conditioned by earlier experiences to check out the edges of the woods for enemy soldiers hiding there before he ascended high enough to be visible.

Sure enough, my dad spotted VC snipers. This time, however, he was able to call up nearby artillery. A US Army soldier, who sounded a lot like a young kid, responded and my father quickly told him where he was located.

"You see those guys sitting out on those hills?" he asked. "I'm flying awfully low and I've got to get out before I get caught in their crosshairs." He had to trust that this artilleryman, as young as he sounded, knew what he was doing. And thankfully he did.

The boyish voice on the other end of the radio commanded firmly, "Do not climb."

As my dad explained to me, "The first shot was fired by our guys. I was told to maintain altitude at full throttle. Basically, the artillery unit had to mark the target with a small gun—something ranging between a 105 and 155 howitzer. After they scored that first shot, they had to hit the other side too."

That's when the young artilleryman repeated again, "Do not climb."

They were firing over my dad's plane now. The next shot was definitely from a 155 because in my father's words, "It came with a helluva dust."

With those two hits, my dad's new best friend in artillery located the enemy unit and the next words he heard from him were, "Meet your power." My dad was about to jam the plane when the kid shouted several more times, "Do not climb! Do not climb!" Miraculously, he was able to stay in position at that low level for three and a half minutes. *Three and a half minutes!* Even I know that's a long time in a little bird-dog airplane that only flies one hundred miles per hour. That speed is nowhere near fast enough to hightail it out of a hot spot like that when you are right at tree-top level, unless of course you've got the kind of targeted artillery support behind you that he did.

After what seemed like forever to even my incredibly patient father, the artilleryman gave the okay for him to climb and then put him on another heading to get him back to base safely. I suspect that my dad doesn't like to tell this story because it took five guns and the explosions of their fuel carriers to take out that enemy unit. He could see a hellacious cloud of smoke in the sky behind him and he knew that a lot of enemy lives were lost that day to save his.

One thing every serviceman and -woman knows is that you can't go it alone in war. You are reliant on other people doing their jobs and they are reliant on you doing yours. In that way, everyone is someone else's reinforcement. Nations also understand this, which is why they seek to develop allies. And militaries plan for this, which is why they train troops to have each other's backs—or as they say, "have each other's six." It's also why they develop elite teams of soldiers with exemplary skills to preempt challenges or to come to the rescue when times get *really* tough. These elite teams, of course, are called Special Forces.

Many people think that it's these warriors' physical abilities that make them so exceptional, but they must be mentally agile and tough and in some cases academically accomplished too. Green Berets, for instance, are able to speak foreign languages like a native, and are fluent in all kinds of advanced technologies. Depending upon their occupational specialty, they've aced weapons, communications, medical and engineering training, and they've been schooled in operations and a wide variety of different survival, escape, resistance, and evasion techniques. But most important, they have to have a rock-solid moral character. Special Forces, in general, must reflect the best attributes and values of the military wherever they are sent. They are often a fleeting presence, emerging only at the times or in the situations when their uncommon skills and fortitude are needed. It takes enormous commitment, courage, and personal responsibility to knowingly rush into a crisis to save others.

Although that artilleryman who effectively saved my father's life was not part of an actual special operations unit, he was my dad's "special force" on that day, stepping in with speed and skill just when it was needed. My father never saw him again, but you can bet he never forgot him.

WHO'S GOT *YOU* COVERED?

When I was very young, my dad shared something with me that he used to tell the battalions he led. As I watched him shave in the early morning one day he said, "The people in your life have an expiration date. You will lose some through death, attrition, their own desires to do greater things, and a host of other reasons. Your ability to let go of them is as important as whom you choose to hang on to. You only have so much space and energy. You have a finite amount of time because you are human. You have limited resources because time is among the materials you must work with. So make sure you have the right people around you to get the things done that you need to get done. And remember that most of us are only with each other one mission at a time. Gain the most from them and be the most with them for as long as is appropriate and successful."

It was an important message about staying focused and having a squad around you that can help you reach excellence. The power of his words has stayed with me ever since. I still have the journal I wrote them in.

The simple truth is that we all need support to achieve our goals and if we don't consider and line up people in our lives who possess the wisdom, skills, moral fiber, and intention to be there for us when we need them most, we may not thrive and survive the way we hope to. Knowing who your allies and special forces are, and by contrast, knowing your enemies and detractors too—the people who intentionally or unintentionally can harm you or impede your progress—is vitally important.

BROTHERS AND SISTERS IN ARMS

Even before I learned how to invite special forces into my life, two such support people appeared on their own. It was during a time when my father was deployed with a company under provisional command. As an officer within the Aviation division of the Army, he was tasked with a wide variety of special missions, including delivering crucial battle plans to eager officers who were awaiting them, transporting wounded soldiers to safety and enemy combatants to detention, extracting long-range reconnaissance patrol units from behind enemy lines, and flying other troops and munitions to and from wherever they were needed most. His technical expertise was in high demand as well. He was known for being able to repair and replace the armaments, avionics, and engines of virtually every kind of aircraft that came back to base damaged, even if he had to improvise. We never knew the nature of his missions when they were occurring, but we knew he would be engaged in this one for a while. Meanwhile my mother and I were living in a nice house in Dallas, Texas, that he had found for us before he shipped off.

On one quiet evening while he was away, someone set off an explosive charge on the exterior wall of our home. The blast it created rocked the entire place, causing the TV to fly across the living room and the photos mounted on that wall to fall and shatter. The shock and damage it caused would have frightened anyone, but it was an especially scary experience for a five-year-old child. While neither of us was physically harmed, we were both terrified to remain there.

My mother wrote to tell my father about what happened but she knew it might take weeks to hear back from him. Fortunately for us, my uncles Ronnie and Tim—Dad's younger brothers—swooped in to help. They mobilized other members of the family to relocate us immediately. My dad's uncle Syria Hulin drove down from Malakoff, Texas, to help move us and our belongings to a safer home in Singing Hills, near Oak Cliff, Texas. They chose the new home because it was closer to where my uncles and my father's mother and stepfather lived. They knew they could keep a closer eye on us there.

When my dad finally received my mom's letter, he drove all the way to headquarters in Saigon to request a leave. The Red Cross agreed to look into the matter but denied his request a few days later. The colonel my father reported to wasn't present at the time or he surely would have granted it. Others were permitted leaves for far less serious matters. Whether his request was denied because he was needed where he was, or because we had moved already by then, is hard to say. But you can only imagine the stress and anxiety he felt under the circumstances. He arranged to use one of the high-frequency radios to contact my mother late one night. Sitting on the back of a truck, he patiently waited for his call to be patched through to a station out in the Pacific then relayed to us in Texas. This delay only seemed to reinforce the nine-thousand-mile distance between them. My mother was still disturbed by the event when they finally spoke, but she assured him that his family had taken care of us and that we had moved to new accommodations already. She didn't want him to worry. She kept up a brave front for him well after that initial call, writing to him daily and including prayers in her letters.

Although my mother filed a police report, no one was ever charged with the crime. Apparently, the officers had no leads. Who did this or why they did it remains a mystery, but my family always suspected that it was racially motivated. Discontent with Dallas's school zones was brewing. A black man named Sam Tasby and twenty other plaintiffs were getting ready to file a landmark class action lawsuit in federal court. They objected to bussing their children to all black Dallas Independent School District schools when they lived so close to white schools. Some residents were highly critical of the suit, claiming that Dallas had already implemented enough zoning changes years before, due to the Supreme Court ruling in the Brown v. Board of Education case. But in fact, Dallas schools were still largely segregated. After hearing the Tasby case, the presiding judge decided in favor of the plaintiffs saying that they had indeed been victims of racial prejudice. He ordered immediate statewide desegregation. Many white families moved out of Dallas shortly after that order. Given the general tensions in the community, my family's suspicions that this explosion might have been an act of racial bias were understandable.

I had no recollection of the incident at my home, but when I heard about it later, the story resonated with me so much that I somehow knew I was an eyewitness to the event, even if I didn't retain the memory of it because of my young age. What I do recall after that time is always feeling as if my uncles were my prized special forces—that for as long as they possibly could, they would be there for my family and me.

Later in my life, I was lucky enough to have another fine person come to my aid during a difficult time. Montel Williams, the famous radio and TV talk show host, happened to be the special force in this case. As some of you know, an ex-boyfriend of mine had violently stalked me for several years beginning in the spring of 1993. This ex broke into my home and forcibly assaulted me. He menaced my neighbors, colleagues, office- and apartment-building workers, and he actively staked out my male friends and companions. Despite my having a restraining order against him, his obsession escalated. He repeatedly entered my home when I wasn't there to steal personal items and leave reminders that he had access to me no matter how often I changed my locks. He not only harassed me in two states, he followed me to an out-of-town convention in Illinois where he thought my order of protection didn't apply. After doing a little jail time, he persisted and even got past police, security guards, and a private detective I hired as a bodyguard. I was naturally terrified of him. To help myself rebound and to guide other women going through the same horrific experience, I wrote a book about it and appeared on numerous talk shows. I was still very nervous about being so exposed, but I knew I had to push past those fears if my life was ever going to return to normal.

On the day I appeared on *The Montel Williams Show*, Montel did something I hadn't anticipated. He looked squarely at the camera and spoke directly to my assailant and stalker. He said, "I know who you are." Then he called him out, right there on live TV. He told him in no uncertain terms that if he tried to pull anything again—if he did me any harm whatsoever—that he would personally wreak havoc on him. What you need to know is that Montel is a former naval officer. In that moment, he spoke with all the moral authority and might that someone with that training and experience has. It had to scare any offender, not just mine, into thinking twice about what they were doing.

I cannot tell you how much trust in others was restored for me in that moment. That someone I did not know very well would put himself out there like that for me was both inspiring and comforting. In your moment of need people will pleasantly surprise you. People who have no obligation to help you will step up and do the right thing. They will invite themselves to be a member of your squad, and believe me, you will gratefully accept their help.

#SQUADGOALS

As fortunate as I was in the instances I just described, none of us should rely on luck. To craft the life we want, accomplish the missions we have in mind, and assure our well-being, we need to pick the right team to be at our side. I often call this team of personal special forces *my inner circle* or *my squad.* There are others whom I will invite to help me out on a project-by-project basis, but members of this elite corps are people I trust to be dedicated to me, not just dedicated to our shared objective.

All the football players on a team competing to win the Super Bowl, for example, have a common goal: To become champions. But not everyone on the team will be excited to see you emerge as the MVP. There will be some who recognize that your consistent game and team leadership have earned you that honor and will push for you, but there will also be others who won't want to see you get that reward instead of them. The kinds of people I want at my side are those who see and want the same things for me that *I* want for myself.

When I think about the people who fought alongside my father, I see people who were committed to him as much as to the mission. The fellow airmen he had around him in the sky weren't just dedicated to the goal of winning the war; they were dedicated to bringing each other back alive. You want people like that around you—people who you can trust with your life.

When I first selected the members of my inner circle, I asked myself the following questions. I want you to do it too. It will help you figure out who is really in your camp. Read the following aloud:

1. Whom do I count on when it comes to making big decisions in my life? I'm not just talking about whom I bounce ideas off of or whom I compare my options with, but whom do I chart my course for greater self-improvement with?
2. Whom do I trust to tell my dreams and goals to?
3. Whom would I call in a time of need—no matter what the hour, day or night?
4. Whom would I allow to call *me* and expect me to be there for them no matter what time day or night?
5. Who tells me the truth no matter how they think it will make me feel?

Remember, the only way someone qualifies is if they meet all of the criteria. No exceptions.

It is such a selective process that you will likely discover, as I did, that there are only a few people who make the list. But the length of that list doesn't matter as long as the people on it happen to be those like your favorite aunt—someone who doesn't necessarily excel at math but knows you well enough to see you're a rocket scientist and wants to help you fulfill your dream of actually becoming one. Someone who will drop off a home-cooked meal at your place so you can maintain your strength while you're studying for exams. Someone who will drive you to and from important interviews, and who will wait for you in the car until you're done. I'm talking about someone who will hang with you and pray when you're having a moment and need some greater guidance. I'm talking about that special someone who will get out and push the limo, and not just expect a ride in it.

Don't be concerned that there are only a few people with that kind of character, heart, and commitment around. The number of Navy SEALs who exist in the world are far fewer than the rest of us. As an example of how quality trumps quantity, it took just about a couple dozen SEAL Team Six members to cleanse the earth of the bloodthirsty terrorist Osama bin Laden. When you have really dedicated people on the job, you don't need that many.

The military calls our Special Forces the "tip of the spear" for a reason. How much of anything do you think you can fit on the tip of something so sharp? Not much, right? But look at the back end of that spear—at the spear's handle. There's a lot more room there for people to hang on—and the more people that are hanging on, the greater the chance that some will be prone to error and distraction. As you move down toward the tip—the part that is pointed directly at its target—there's only room for the best. That's how Special Forces work in the military and that's how I want them to work in my inner circle. There should be no room for error. No room for anybody who doesn't belong.

By the way, the motivational speaker Jim Rohn had an interesting theory. He suggested that our personalities are the average of the five people we spend the most time with. Essentially, the influence of those nearest and dearest to us shapes our values, choices, and behaviors to the point where we develop a shared set of ideals. In other words, our thinking rubs off on each other. If this is true, we have even more reason to choose our company wisely. We must surround ourselves with only the best of the best.

Satisfied that I had identified the members of my squad, the next step for me was to formally enlist those people—to invite them into my inner circle. The military's success is largely based on everyone knowing their role. My squad needed to know that I have expectations of them and what those expectations are. It's easier to do than you might think as you are basically extending the ultimate compliment. Just be specific about what you need, offer your equal support in return, and really mean it when you tell that person you will be there for him or her.

This conscious effort to attract supportive people into my life has increased my sense of security, multiplied my joy, magnified my faith in others, fueled my endeavors, and enabled me to do more with that "finite amount of time" my father spoke of. It has also given me great satisfaction to support others in return.

BY INVITATION ONLY

Now that you've asked all the right questions and made a list of those you can count on, it's time for you to extend the invitations. You may want to follow the script below when making your ask, or you can write your own. Mine is offered here to give you some guidance:

I've recently had an epiphany in my life. I have some things I need to do to make sure I'm living out God's purpose for me here on earth and that means I can't waste my time or His. Since I tend to pray for direction, I want to follow that Divine direction with everything I've got. It's about taking my life's mission to the next level. I'm going to need some extraordinary people around me to rise. I need your positivity, support, and push when I begin to doubt myself. Please know that I extend the same kind of support to you in return.

Yes, you read that last line correctly. If you are asking someone to be in your inner circle you should be prepared for the arrangement to be reciprocal. Given all they will do for you, I am sure you will find pleasure in returning the favors.

Now, if all of a sudden you're panicked because you've started thinking about the many people in your life who could possibly ask this kind of commitment from you, take a deep breath. It's likely that you won't be called in every time help is needed. Many times, people's special forces change with each assignment. They will call up resources for different projects from pretty much anywhere in their life depending upon the task and the kind of support skills needed. In other words, you may have a very short deployment. The best way for me to explain this is to say that I'm blessed to have friends whom I've known for a very long time. Friends I don't see very often, but who would happily be there for me if I picked up the phone tomorrow and asked them to be. They are friends for whom I would do the same thing. They're solid in my life and I'm solid in theirs. If you've been clutch for someone you care about in a pinch like that, then you've already done special-forces duty. Trust that you've got this.

Not Everyone Makes the Cut

What you will likely find is that this whole process of selecting members of your inner circle is wonderful at helping you separate the wheat from the chaff. You will recognize pretty quickly that some people may be fun to hang around with, but they can eat up a lot of your time and keep you from fulfilling your goals.

You may also discover people who don't belong in your life at all, let alone in your inner circle. Having been stalked before, I genuinely hope you never encounter enemies of your own. Sometimes it is difficult to tell who will turn into one until it is too late, but taking inventory like this may trigger some early warning signs. The most dangerous opponents will make it their business to know everything about the party they wish to harm. If you don't know enough about them, you could be caught off guard. This was true in my case and it is true in war.

In Vietnam, the United States made the tactical error of thinking that our airpower was stronger than the Vietcong's willpower. We believed that they were all fighting for Communism when a great many of them had a far deeper incentive: They were fighting *against us*. Not only did we fail to learn more about their motivation, drive, and resourcefulness, we also grossly miscalculated what they knew about us. As former prisoners of war from that era would tell you, they used extreme torture on the American soldiers they captured without any regard for them as individuals. Our enemy was focused on getting whatever information they could to help them think more like we did. They understood that that's how one wins—by getting deep inside their opponents' heads.

The United States is fighting a similar kind of foe today as we battle the Islamic State savages. For example, our well-armed forces took the city of Mosul once, only to lose it. And as of the writing of this book, we are taking it back again. What we didn't know at first about this enemy is how they are constantly learning on the battlefield. They employ soldiers—and I mean actually *pay them*—to do nothing else but study their mistakes. Think about that for a second. We are not just fighting them; we are fighting their constantly evolving expert judgment. They are a *psychologically metastasizing enemy*. This is what makes them such a serious threat and such a difficult force to defeat.

Knowing your enemies—seeing them for who they are first—can actually help you protect yourself and avoid future conflict and danger.

Fortunately, though, the worst offenders in most people's daily lives are the friends who just want to sit around and feast on gossip no matter what the circumstances. You know the kind. They love to consume all your energy talking about things they have no business discussing. It's hard sometimes because to the flesh, that feels good, but to the cause, it's deadly. All of us get together occasionally with our friends to chat and we may even talk about someone who's not present, but hopefully we do so with a will toward helping them find a solution to their challenges. Engaging in negative gossip for gossip's sake though—well, that kind of behavior is a problem.

Believe me, I've allowed people into my life at different points who were like a walking tabloid. And what I found is that their chatter rots the brain. Gossip makes people intellectually lazy.

The person who is always analyzing someone else's life instead of his own is not a friend.

I can guarantee you that those who regularly take inventory of what you and others have will *not* be on your special forces short list. You cannot give your dreams to people who want what you have. And you certainly don't want what they have: Mind-numbingly frivolous ideas about what to do with their time.

If you are reading this book, you've got no desire to live life coveting others' good fortune or imagining their downfall. Instead, you desire to live life enjoying your *own* good fortune and sharing it with others.

Your obvious next step is to cut loose the people who pose threats to the fulfillment of your dreams. The military assures its strength by culling the weak links from its forces early on. Those with an outsized ego or those who refuse to give or take help from another recruit can fail training camp. Having troops who are out of step with everyone else in the unit jeopardizes operations and lives. You must learn to think about your squad and missions in similar terms. You can begin by answering the following question with total honesty: Are you spending more than a few minutes a day or a few hours a week with someone who doesn't check off enough boxes on your list?

If your answer is yes, you have some important life renovations to make. You must resolve to create the most perfect environment for success possible because as you begin to fill up your mind and your spirit with the prospects of positive change, those people who are not 100 percent with you will be resistance points for you later on. They will consciously or unconsciously set out on a course that is the total opposite of the one you are trying to navigate. And because you have allowed them in your midst and you've proven that you trust them, you might just listen to them. While you may not have embraced an outright saboteur, you will certainly have invited diversions into your camp.

If you're not spending enough time with the few people in your newly formed inner circle, you can safely assume that you're spending too much time with the people who don't belong. The minute you cut these negative influences out, the more time you'll have to spend with the people whose company you should be in. It's natural law. If I'm no longer hanging out with Sarah, Robin, and Lulu because it turns out they are not my best allies, then I am free to see more of the people who are.

Listen, we all spend time with the people who make them-selves available to us, but quality people don't generally have time to be available for everyone. If they don't feel like they're appre-ciated or they are adding something of value to the world, they pick up their energies and gifts and place them elsewhere. My mother was like that. She'd spend an hour or two with you, but if you weren't a serious person, she'd find a way to spend less and less time with you. She'd love you, but she wasn't going to lavish another precious minute on frivolous activities. Whenever you would call, she'd tell you that she was busy, and she was. Once you trim your list to include only those quality people who are fulfilling your needs, I'm telling you the length of that list will guarantee that you now have all the time in the world to spend with them. Concerned that sounds too selfish? Well it's not. It's actually self-saving. You're preserving yourself for the squad that can help you raise your game to the next level. #squadgoals!

If you want to see a liberating example of how removing dis-tractors from your life can make room for more noble special forces, think about the criminals locked up in jail. For the life of them, they couldn't find God outside the walls of prison because they were surrounded 24–7 by people just like themselves. But as soon as they have to sit alone in a cell for sixteen hours a day, they suddenly find the Lord. Without all those other influences, they finally have time for the one quality Being in their life.

In the end, the hardest part of this exercise for you will not be about finding the time to be with good people. The hardest part of this exercise will actually involve telling those other people that you don't want to spend time with them anymore because they're negative forces in your life. But it's something you have to do because if you don't, it won't matter what your goals are. It won't matter how you dress or how fit you are. It won't matter how much integrity you intend to unleash on the world. And if you have any issues you have not dealt with yet, I can promise you the wrong people will exploit those weaknesses because they just can't help themselves. When you have people around you who give off negativity, you'll spend more time fending off strife than pursuing success and enjoying life.

So how do you actively unfriend the people in your life who don't make the list?

Once again, I defer to the common sense of the military. There is no room for error when conveying a message in wartime. Be direct and be brief. The conversation could start something like this:

I've recently had an epiphany in my life. Some changes are necessary if I'm going to live out God's purpose for me here on this earth, and that means I can't waste my time or His. Since I tend to pray for direction, I want to follow that Divine guidance with everything I've got. You are really busy with all the things that you are doing right now and supporting me in the way I need to be supported is going to be an imposition in your life. So why don't we get to the point where we spend some real quality time together every now and then, but be less everyday people with each other. I need something different and as I pursue it, I don't want to be a burden in your life.

If you think you can't deliver this message, think again. All of us have had a crush on somebody in our past who has found the words to break up with us, right? Well then, we all have the language at our disposal to do the same thing. This is not your first rodeo. Remember, that is essentially what you're doing—you're respectfully breaking up with somebody. I promise you, you can put some distance between yourself and this other person and not be a jerk about it. But you cannot walk away from that conversation without selling the determination you have to start anew. This step is critical to achieving success. Surrounding yourself with the wrong people is a form of self-abuse.

Which brings me to another important point: Part of making a special-forces arrangement work entails knowing how dedicated you are too. If you have allowed someone into your inner circle because they have inordinate faith in your abilities, that's great. But if you let that same person convince you to go out with her instead of putting finishing touches on a presentation that's due the next day because, as she says, "you're good enough to wing it," then you have to examine your own level of determination. The more leeway you give to the people who are closest to you—the more rule breaking you permit them to do in your presence— the more you have to question your own seriousness. If your dedication is that easily broken, that's not really on them; it's on you. If there are temptations of your own that are deterring you from fulfilling your goals, you will have to stop and address those temptations right now. But if you find, after some soul-searching, that you are still serious, then you must fire any distractor in your midst immediately. They will not be there for you in the long haul.

Something I once heard Mark Cuban—the hugely successful entrepreneur, philanthropist, investor, owner of the NBA's Dallas Mavericks, and costar of television's *Shark Tank*—say was that the one regret he's had over the years is that he did not fire people the moment it popped into his head that he should. And he's right. People who suck all the resources from you are like those bad employees. To keep them from destroying what you are building, you have to let them go.

Another important reason for letting distractors go is that sometimes they may be keeping other truly committed people from joining your team. Remember, no one of quality will follow you into the heavens if you are flying in a flock of vultures.

MAYBE ANOTHER TIME

One further thought regarding people who were part of your home team, but who may have fallen away because at one time or another your goals and theirs differed: Always leave yourself open to happy surprises. Somewhere down the line, after they or you have grown, you may reenter each other's lives again. I have a dear friend whom I was out of touch with for many years. She made some choices at one point in her life that I wouldn't have made for myself. Because of these differences, she chose to part ways. It hurt because I love her, but I am happy to say that more recently she has come around again and has invited me back into her inner circle. When I asked her what changed she said, "I looked up one day and the friends that I had were not quality like you. I knew that that could only be a reflection on me. And besides, I missed you." I missed her too and am happy to have her back.

But that's not always the case with these things. When you live in the public eye, as I do, it can often seem as if you've hit the lottery when it comes to friends. Any amount of recognition acts like a magnet, attracting all sorts of people to you. Because enjoying the company of so many newfound friends can be a distraction, I've had to practice the art of the breakup on a number of occasions.

One kind of breakup I find particularly disheartening is with people who try to gain something from their association with me at my expense. An instance like this occurred on a recent evening when I was enjoying a leisurely dinner with some extended family and friends. One of our dinner guests decided to loudly indicate to a restaurant packed full of patrons that I was present. She name-dropped in such a way that suddenly a relaxing night off for me and everyone else at the table turned into one where we were all talking about work. A few well-meaning diners and Fox News fans approached us to say hello, which was lovely. But when the dinner ended, my husband—who is my number one special force—knew that the attention-seeker at our table did not belong in our inner circle, at least not for the rest of that evening. He suggested that we continue on to another location for drinks after dinner. We did so by ourselves.

Distancing yourself from members of your work family is

sometimes called for as well. Handling these distractors requires even more nuanced and practiced skills. The best advice I can give you is not to engage outside of the office with potential attention grabbers if you can help it. You may also be paired with someone on a project who is a notorious time waster. Under those circumstances you must do your best to be a team player, but when the day is done, take off your Louis Vuittons, put on a pair of Skechers, and keep moving. You can kiss that person on each cheek because you are grateful for the work they did, but don't stop walking. They are paid to cooperate with you and to do their part for the company to succeed, but they do not necessarily have the same incentive to be your friend outside of work.

In some businesses, especially television news, the kind of gossip I alluded to earlier runs rampant. That may be true in your business too. Even if you're not privy to all the buzz because you tend to shy away from it, you can tell by your colleagues' body language whether or not they're quality people. I call those who engage in that kind of unproductive office talk "the huddles." They cluster together and speak in low tones until you get closer and then the tone suddenly shifts. Instantly, there's boisterous laughter as if they're covering for what was just said. You have to wonder what the rumblings in the huddle are all about. If these people are not assembling to talk about ratings, sales figures, or some new feature of the company's business plan, then their babble probably isn't something I need to be bothered with. Engaging in that behavior would not just be harmful to me, it would be harmful to the work too. You should really try to let go of these kinds of people outside of your workday. Lace your integrity right through this particular channel of your life, recognizing that some people are with us for just one mission. If you release them in a dignified manner, they may even learn something valuable from the experience.

Of course, *recruiting* special forces on the job can be just as complicated as avoiding troublesome distractors. People may assure you in any number of ways that they don't want the career path or success that you have, but beware. They may know somebody else who wants it and their allegiance to that somebody else may be stronger than it is to you. They may very well be part of this other person's inner circle. So my best advice to you is to seek special forces who have established their worth long ago. They can give generously of their knowledge to you because they are so rich in experience they don't feel threatened, nor do they need to be opportunistic in your company.

One of the greatest gifts my father gave to me was an introduction to Barbara Rodgers. For those of you who may not know her, she was one of the most recognizable newscasters on CBS 5 Eyewitness News in San Francisco for nearly thirty years. She is an award-winning anchor, reporter, and show host who has interviewed many, many newsmakers, community leaders, and celebrities. Her work earned her countless honors, including seven Emmy Awards, five Excellence in Journalism Awards from the National Association of Black Journalists, as well as awards for reporting from the Associated Press, United Press International, The Peninsula Press Club, and The Society of Professional Journalists. We had a fabulous conversation, and while our paths only crossed that one time, she continued to inspire me over the years through her great work and my memory of her grace and positivity. She is the caliber of people whose company we should be seeking.

A MATTER OF CHARACTER

One of the earliest and most memorable lessons I learned about the people I should and shouldn't invite into my circle occurred when I was in junior high school. I arrived home one day with several new friends. My mother hadn't met them before, but I thought they were all cool. One in particular had a really bold sense of style. I loved fashion. We bonded over that, and while I noticed that she could be mean to some of the other girls at times, she was never that way with me.

We hadn't been home for very long when my mother pulled me aside and said, "If you don't get those women out of this house right now, I'm going to do something that will really embarrass you," I was stunned. First, because she called these girls "women" when we were only fourteen years old and second, because she had never said anything like that to me before in my entire life. I had friends over for playdates all the time, and she was always so gracious to them. But for some reason, she really didn't want these girls anywhere near me.

I remember protesting, "But Mom, they're here now. I can't just send them home."

"Fine," she said between pursed lips. "But when this is over we're going to talk about who you allow next to you and who you keep away. People will judge you based on the other kids you're hanging out with. Opportunities are given and taken away because of the company you keep. More importantly, these girls can affect how you make decisions."

Just when I thought she was finished, she added, "I'm trying to teach you one set of values and you're hanging out with a girl who I'm pretty sure is already sexually active."

I was flabbergasted. "Whoa. Who? How do you know?" I stammered. "I really don't think so, Mom. I mean, we're really young."

Later that evening we talked more. She reminded me that I didn't have a curfew because she trusted me. "But I don't trust them," she said. "So if you are with those girls outside of this house, I am telling you, you will be home early and you will have more rules and more parameters than usual."

As time went on I couldn't really hang out with these friends anymore because while I was not grounded in the traditional sense, I started having more and more chores piled on me. Every time I told my mother that I was meeting the girls at the mall on a Saturday afternoon, she would say, "Well before you go and do that, I really need you to iron that pile of pillowcases. Don't leave until they're finished." *Iron the pillowcases!* How crazy is that?

In retrospect of course, I recognize those insane tasks as the love of a good mother. Her mission was to instill good judgment in me. She wanted me to be around others whose parents were guiding them in the same way that she and my dad were trying to guide me. "How engaged are their parents?" she asked. "It's nine o'clock in the evening and I haven't received a phone call from them wondering where their child is. If you were over at somebody else's house at nine P.M., you can be sure I'd be checking up on you." Of course, we didn't have cell phones at that time, so parents were always calling each other to check on the safety of their kids. A lack of a call from a friend's mom was a pretty conspicuous thing.

My mother trusted me right up until I came home with those girls. When she saw my misplaced friendship, it gave her pause for concern, so she set out to make sure that nothing would sidetrack me from doing all the things I needed to do in order to become the person that I am today—someone who has enjoyed so many blessings and wonderful experiences because my parents helped me remain focused on the end goal.

My mother was also acting very much like a military spouse. She was reminding me that I was a brat. No pun intended. The company I was keeping didn't reflect well on me. But even more important, it didn't reflect well on my dad or on her. When you are the child of a military officer you are one of his special forces. That means you live by the same values he does. My mother lived by those core values too. She was highly respected on base. She chaired committees, hosted welcome parties for new families, ran support groups for those whose loved ones were deployed, and organized fund-raisers for a variety of charities, particularly those that helped children in need. Most other brats will tell you that at some point in their young lives they also had to take stock of their friendships. Having anyone other than quality people around you meant that you didn't have enough time to support your own goals or the incredibly serious goals of your parents.

Occasionally, I'll look at a pillowcase and smile. My mother sure knew how to make a point.

Rule #2

DEAL WITH YOUR DEMONS

There is a story I once heard about a recruit who was so flustered by the demands and chaos of boot camp he couldn't do anything right. Every inspection he failed, every repetitive task he blundered, every small or large infraction he committed led to additional tasks for the whole unit. Finally, his drill instructor was so frustrated he made this recruit carry his mask around with him wherever he went. The point was to remind him of how he was sucking the air out of the experience for everyone else. Since I've heard other clever variations on this theme, I don't know if the story is apocryphal—a military legend passed down to keep recruits who are not pulling their weight from embarrassing themselves in the same way—but exaggerated or not, the point is that every serviceman and -woman needs to be able to do the same things the rest of the unit is doing in order for all of them to survive and thrive.

The exercises recruits are put through during training—as arbitrary as they may seem at times—are actually designed to help break troops of their bad habits so they can replace them with lifesaving ones. They are intended to teach discipline and the importance of acting in unison with each other. Any bad habit that prevents a recruit from doing this is something they seriously need to wrestle with and overcome, because if they don't, they run the risk of jeopardizing *everyone's* success and safety in the field, not just their own.

As it happened, my father bypassed the whole boot-camp-from-hell experience. After a quick assessment of his abilities at Fort Hood in Killeen, Texas, during his junior year in college, it was decided that once he had his degree he would go directly to Officer Training School (OTS) alongside West Point officers and other distinguished military graduates. He's too modest to say it, but when the Army saw that he lacked the bad habits they try to break in new recruits and possessed so many of the admirable qualities they try to instill in them, they were eager to have him join their ranks.

After OTS, he became a platoon leader. That's where he helped so many young men learn to swap out their worst habits for far better ones. Despite how dedicated and bright the non-commissioned officers he trained were, he told me that the most frequent and detrimental habit he had to break in them was a "certain kind of selfishness." He explained, "In their desire to be the best that they could possibly be, they focused solely on their own performance and not on that of the collective team. But winning requires the *whole unit* to be dominant in its mission ability. To remedy the problem, these young men have to learn to love the man next to him as soon as possible. They have to learn to do things together or the unit will never become proficient. In this business of field training, they have to learn that *your eyes are not just your eyes. Your eyes are the eyes of the guy that is next to you and next to him.* They have to discover that through these exercises, *you learn to see again. You learn to see together.*"

When service members look back on their early training experiences, they all admit what an important role strict drill instructors and wise platoon leaders played in their growth, transformation, and readiness for success in battle. The methods they used may have varied, but their objective was always the same: To help you identify and correct the behaviors, habits, and beliefs that could potentially get in the way of mission success.

FORCE OF HABIT

Most of us are like young recruits. We are eager to achieve success, but we have certain habits, quirks, and character flaws that need to be addressed before that can happen. Maybe those habits are not so visible to others—or even to yourself at times—but scratch the surface and you'll see them lurking there, forming a thin layer of resistance between you and your goals. I call the worst of these habits "demons" because a lot of times we don't recognize how bad their influence is until they've already created some trouble for us. I devised the "Deal with Your Demons" rule to remind me to be on the lookout for these unwanted habits, to challenge them before they ever grow to be too powerful, and to replace them with more constructive habits that will assure my success.

TIME FOR A CHANGE

It's difficult to imagine now, but throughout the first half of my life I was chronically late for *everything*. Maybe you or someone you know has the same challenge. I would always pass it off as no big deal, joking that I was even born late, having arrived two weeks after my due date. My tardiness was so persistent, my grade school teachers noted it in my childhood report cards. My high school friends automatically built in an extra twenty minutes for me no matter where we were going, until one day they figured out that the time they spent waiting could be better spent having fun. From that point on they left ahead of me and hoped that I'd catch up.

There were times when this awful habit disappointed my mother too. I would come late to events she hosted for the other military families. I never meant for it to seem as if I didn't care about our friends and neighbors enough to be on time, but my mother made me see how it could appear that way. In fact, she was the first to identify this shortcoming of mine as a "little demon." She even warned me to be careful because habits like these can control us if we let them.

As always, she was right. When I went to college, that little demon seemed to grow two heads. Now it wasn't just letting people down; it was also costing my parents and me a hefty price. Sometime during the first quarter of my freshman year one of my professors threatened to lower my stellar grade in his course if I didn't make it to class on time. At first I thought that he was overreacting and that it would all just blow over, but it didn't. I finally told my mother and she was not pleased. College wasn't free or cheap. She and my father had planned and worked hard to be able to pay for it, and I had also worked hard to earn good grades. She suggested that I draw a line down the center of a piece of paper and list all the pros of being late on one side and all the cons on the other. Guess what. There were no pros. I had to own up to my behavior and do something about it quickly. I compromised and picked three manageable things I could arrive on time for and focused on those. They were my classes, exams, and my favorite social events. I'd have to work on being prompt for everything else some other time.

Of course, "some other time" eventually caught up with me. In the same way that I had set some priorities about what I would *never* be late for in college, I determined that in my professional life I would *never* be late for a newscast. My little demon knew there was no negotiation on this point. I stuck to the plan and it remains a deal breaker to this day. However, something my news director said to me one afternoon made me realize that picking just one thing to be consistently on time for was not good enough.

He said, "Harris, I get that you'll be there for the news, but will you show up for life?"

His question stopped me in my tracks. He was clearly irritated and had finally decided to confront me on the subject. He continued, "You know, we planned a group lunch for the people in the newsroom this week and you were fifteen minutes late, so you missed my opening remarks. I realize that it wasn't breaking news, but I have to ask, are you *always* late like that?" I think he might have thought that I was just disrespecting *him*.

As you can imagine, that event was a turning point for me— even more so than the other incidents. This time, the potential consequences for me seemed far more serious. I began to see my worst habit as the demon I'd been warned about. If I wasn't careful, it could prevent me from doing the kind of work I believed I was born to do. It could actually derail my career.

The great irony about my persistent lateness is that I love watches and always have. I've collected large, vintage, and fancy timepieces for years. As a young child I even used to wear my dad's watch around the house. He left it lying on the dresser alongside his dog tags when he changed out of his uniform or went to sleep. It's not as if I didn't know what time it was all those years; it was that I couldn't resist the urge to take one more minute to do one last thing. But now I somehow understood the danger of that urge. If left unchecked it could ruin my future in a business I had wanted to be in all my life—a business where I showed real promise for success.

I knew right then and there that I had to rid myself of this awful habit and replace it with a whole new set of good ones. I had to be prompt everywhere I went and I had to direct some of the awareness that made me such a good journalist in the direction of the people I worked with. I knew what I needed from them to do a good job, but what did they need from me to do their job better? What could we do for each other to take us all to a ratings win? An Emmy? A Peabody? I wondered if when my news director gave his speech, he shared thoughts on his vision for the team going forward. It was now very clear that being late to that luncheon meant I missed more than just the appetizers; I may have missed information that could enhance the way I perform—the way we *all* perform together.

The other irony about my tardiness was that I lived on a military base, yet I never thought about the way our soldiers tell time—or what that way of telling time says about the importance of being where you are supposed to be *when* you are supposed to be there. Think about it: To be sure there is no confusion about whether an operation begins in the day or at night, the military adopted use of the twenty-four-hour clock. You cannot confuse 12:00 A.M. with 12:00 P.M. when you think of midnight as 0000 hours and noon as 1200 hours. This small but significant innovation not only ensures that the troops are in sync, but it also emphasizes how important being there for each other is—on time, fully present, and ready.

Although I was *taught* on countless occasions and in countless different ways that my tardiness would bite me in the butt if I let it, I only truly *learned* that lesson when being late all the time came close to doing that. This is what I mean when I say, "Deal with your demons." We all have a sense of what our worst habits are. We dismiss them because they seem perfectly harmless at a distance. But you must consider not just how your bad habits obstruct your way, but also how they can be detrimental to the goals and resources of the people you care about. It was when my tardiness threatened my parents' hard-earned money and my college grades that I woke up to it. It was when it started to interfere with my professional life, including others who supported my work, that my eyes were fully opened. Only when you see the threat your demon poses clearly enough can you begin to break its hold on you.

I am proud to say that when this rule about knowing and overcoming my demons really clicked for me, my perspective shifted. I aimed to show up early and not just for newscasts. As I've mentioned in this book, today I cohost an ensemble show that dominates its time slot because our panelists work well as a team. We've developed a wonderful rhythm by being attentive and drawing upon each other's strengths and knowledge. *In other words, we've cultivated good habits.* The same dynamic exists among my producing team on *Outnumbered Overtime with Harris Faulkner.*

Of course, I won't sugarcoat things for you. I still have to actively remind myself to keep an eye on the time every morning when my husband, daughters, and I are all rushing around to get to school, work, or an appointment. But there is something a few hundred yards from my home that serves as a visual reminder for me to stay on track. I live near a ferry dock on the Hudson River. It became famous as the location where Captain Chesley Sullenberger (known to many as "Sully") made an emergency water landing of US Airways flight 1549. You will recall that this plane was disabled by a flock of geese right after takeoff one cold January afternoon in 2009. Now, whenever I look at this dock from my front window, I am inspired by the thought of what the human spirit can do. If Sully could accomplish such a miraculous feat with just seconds to plan for it, then certainly with a little more preparation I can make it to the ferry on time each day.

YOU PLAY LIKE YOU PRACTICE

There is no perfect journey. I find that as the mother of two elementary-school-aged daughters, little demons arise from time to time that I try to catch early. I revisit this rule and find ways to slay those demons in an effort to be a better role model for my girls. I know that one can develop an unwanted habit at any point in life. For instance, how many people addicted to social media could have predicted their struggle five years ago? I'm sure they never imagined a time when they would dine in a restaurant opposite their date and not exchange a word with each other because they couldn't pry themselves away from their iPhones. But today we witness that happening more and more. New trends and technologies emerge and a whole new set of demons appears with them to entice us.

To be sure that no bad habits form or escape my notice and that no benign ones turn into something more (Is eating a lot of chocolate really that bad?), I rely on the trusty principles of boot camp. I use *discipline* and an *abundance of awareness* to my advantage. I check to make certain that I am not backsliding on my vow to get to places on time. I stop and take inventory of the things I've been doing lately and look for patterns. I ask myself how some of these things may be affecting the people around me.

I also take constructive criticism in stride. I consider the source, and if it's coming from someone I love, care about, and/or respect, then I know it is being offered because the other person genuinely wants to see me succeed. I've grown to understand and appreciate that others bring a level of objectivity to the conversation, especially if they are people I trust. This is where my special forces come in. I'm sure if they spotted a new habit unfolding, they would be the first to tell me. If it were a good habit, they'd give me a compliment and encourage me to develop it further. If it were not, they'd give me a word of advice.

This whole idea of early detection—remaining alert and aware enough to spot and deal with habits before they ever spiral into something as big as a demon—is really important. It worked for me once in a very significant way.

When I was first starting out in my career I used to be what I call, for lack of a better term, *a noisy listener.* You know, one of those people who interjects to assure others that they're still with them as they tell their story. The type who always says "uh-huh" and "mm-hmm" when they can relate, or even "oof" when they want to let the other person know that they feel their pain. This habit may prove that you're sympathetic when your friend tells you about her latest romantic breakup or your child skins his knee, but it's the kiss of death if you're a news reporter. After you interview enough people at fire scenes, you'll stop doing that real fast because your news clips will never be broadcast.

This was something I did so much as a young person in the field, that it could very well have stalled my prospects for on-camera work or halted it all together. Whenever I'd sit down with my editor to watch the video that my cameraman just shot of me interviewing an eyewitness, I'd find myself feeling deflated within minutes. The editor would invariably say, "You're right on point. You got the scoop, but we can't use the footage because you're talking over it." I'd ask to take another listen and he'd play it back for me. Sure enough, the interview subject would be saying something critical just as I was voicing my understanding or sympathy. The audio was never clear enough to air.

The same would sometimes happen off camera too. I might have been tracking down crucial information—maybe someone was reading the telephone number of an important contact aloud for me to write down. If I was saying "uh-huh" as they were saying the next number, I missed it. That was especially troublesome when I only had seconds to get that information and the person relaying it to me had already hung up the phone.

You can bet I worked really hard to break that habit. Now after I ask a question, I remain silent until I'm sure my interviewees have finished their response. I don't say "uh-huh" or "mm-hmm" anymore because I'm trying to hear every word they are saying and if I'm speaking, then I can't do that. Similarly, when young journalists are interviewing me and I get interrupted more than once in two sentences, I stop answering. What I have to say in that situation can't be heard over their voices. I often tell them later why I do this so they can learn the same lesson I had to learn without going through similar frustrations.

This is exactly what I mean when I say, "Deal with your demons." You must recognize them and by extension work to be sure you conquer them. This particular habit could have stalled my career—or worse, halted it all together. But because I was aware enough to identify the problem, heed my editor's comments, and change my ways, I not only avoided trouble, I actually became a far better reporter.

TAKING THE MESSAGE PUBLIC

Whenever I talk with my brat friends about my "Deal with Your Demons" rule we always have a good laugh. For the most part, brats are some of the best-behaved children you will ever meet. They grow up surrounded by disciplined and aware people all the time. Their parents and others on base model these qualities so brats tend to learn them by both osmosis and steady reinforcement. But we all remember rebelling in little ways, especially around the time when our loved one was deployed. Rules would sometimes get lax around the house because our mom was doing double duty, assuming our dad's role in addition to her own while he was gone. We might find ourselves stretching our bedtimes, delaying or not doing our homework, skipping a chore to hang out at the bowling alley on base just to blow off some steam, and though fast food wasn't as prevalent then as it is today, we would relax our diet and indulge in ice cream and pizza a little bit more. But sooner or later brats catch themselves and straighten up. We don't believe in pity parties. We pretty much pick ourselves up and move forward before any of these indulgences threaten to become lasting habits or demons.

Given the example of our parents' service to country, a lot of us brats grow up pursuing careers in fields that also call out, address, and/or tackle challenging behaviors and demons in our own society and in others around the world. A disproportionate number of us enter the military, become police officers, social workers, teachers, foreign service workers, and some—like me— become journalists.

A lot of my job is about focusing the public on behavioral patterns, recurring challenges, and thorny issues we collectively need to pay attention to in order to keep moving in a good direction as individuals, patriots, and as global citizens. Although it is difficult, there are times when I have to call out growing concerns in institutions I deeply care about, including the military, precisely because I care about them. I know that if we wish these institutions to continue to serve us as well as they have in the past, we have to mind their demons the same way we mind our own.

One of several demons I see society and the military currently wrestling with is the issue of how to better attend to the health needs of our veterans. This has been a challenge dating back to my father's day. The decades' worth of medical advances made between World War II and the Vietnam era resulted in more troops surviving and returning home with physical injuries that would have previously been life ending. Because Vietnam also engaged our troops in guerrilla-style warfare and in direct confrontations with civilians, our soldiers carried back deep psychological wounds, the likes of which we had never seen or dealt with before. They were traumatized by fighting battles without clear rules, boundaries, or even an identifiable enemy. The further burden of the war's unpopularity at home didn't help. Troops returning with PTSD were very reluctant to call attention to themselves by reaching out for help. To admit that they needed counseling felt like too public a shame to bear. So many of them suffered alone and in silence. Consequently, the suicide rate among veterans spiked. Alcoholism, drug use, and homelessness also rose.

Thankfully, we made considerable progress in the intervening years. We are now more responsive than we once were. A greater number of doctors and civilians understand the ravages of war and have stepped up to help meet the responsibility of caring for our current veterans physically, emotionally, and mentally. We have a broader understanding of PTSD and its treatment.

The work of foundations such as Wounded Warrior Project, Disabled American Veterans Charitable Service Trust, Air Warrior Courage Foundation, and Operation Second Chance also evidences a societal change. These organizations' existence proves a wider public appreciation for our troops and an increased willingness to help them in whatever ways we can.

The challenge, however, is that the situation continues to morph with the new circumstances of war. Tours of duty have increased in number and duration. Even more miraculous surgical and rehabilitative strides have been made. As a great many service members return in need of medical care, the stress on the system *and* on them has become monumental. The conditions these brave soldiers face from day one of their homecoming are grave, challenging, and often insurmountable. Some require daily urgent care visits. Their recovery times stretch on into years. No system can sustain the equivalent of an emergency room visit every day by so many people. As we continue to find new ways to save lives and limbs, we must also find new ways to ensure the quality of our wounded veterans' existence afterward. This is a demon we *all* need to contemplate, innovate around, and resolve swiftly.

We've been a nation at war for more than a decade in places we all largely agreed to be in. There may be some political divide on this matter, but generally there is widespread support among the American people for the troops who went to Iraq and Afghanistan. No one can say for sure, however, what level of support there will be if we have to send more armed men and women back into those countries or into new areas of conflict. With mounting threats every day in Syria and North Korea, we are going to be in a world of hurt if we do not figure this challenge out now. Our health-care facilities will be crippled under the weight of a greater number of troops relying on them.

What compounds this problem is that older vets are living longer too. Those in my dad's generation—and those before his time as well—are in increasing need of medical care that is very different from the care young vets require.

I was intimately impacted by this reality six summers ago when my parents came to visit my husband, two girls, and me at our vacation home in southern Arizona. We were enjoying our leisure time together when my father became ill. He never told us that he'd been having some esophageal problems and was taking prescribed medication to treat the symptoms for quite some time.

As it turned out, the condition was far more serious than he led us to believe. Whereas he usually received medical care on base, we were nowhere near his regular doctors or a VA hospital. Our best option was to send him to Tucson Medical Center (TMC). It was one of the closest facilities, and thankfully it is also one of the best in the country. They used a life flight service to transport him from where we were near the US–Mexican border to their intensive care unit. He spent the next sixty-seven days in a coma. I am happy to say because of their immediate response and excellent treatment he recovered fully. Around the same time as he was convalescing, the media began shedding light on the epic wait times those seeking medical services through the VA were subjected to. I found myself increasingly conflicted that some of our soldiers and officers may not have been getting access to the same kind of care. Reporting shows the issue is not with how well trained and talented the doctors and nurses at VA hospitals are. There is a tremendous amount of talent at our VA hospitals. Rather, the system is burdened by the enormous patient overload they're experiencing, to say nothing of the severity and complexity of injuries and conditions they are dealing with.

The doctors told us that without immediate attention my father would have died. We sadly know some of our veterans have died on waiting lists. The failure to quickly fix this ongoing challenge at the VA is the legacy of the Obama administration, and arguably, of previous presidents from both political parties. We are seeing Americans who have never served react by urging their own congresspeople to do their part with compassionate urgency.

Another perplexing military demon involves the issue of sexual harassment, particularly against women. Of course, the armed services are not alone in their need to address this challenge. All of society is struggling with it. But the military must get its arms around this matter quickly for several reasons. The first is because it's our moral obligation to. All of our troops are entitled to mutual respect. The second is because our troops' ability to trust one another and to act in unison will be eroded if they don't. While most of the people who serve our country uphold military values and treat each other with the dignity that their commitment warrants, those who don't actually threaten our military readiness.

There is much that the military has done during the last few years to improve conditions for women, but sadly the nude-photo-sharing scandal of 2017 took us back a number of steps. I am referring to the marines who explicitly posted images of female troops without their knowledge or permission through a private Facebook page that was later discovered and publicized in the media.

During a 2017 Senate Arms Services Committee hearing on the subject, Republican Senator Mike Rounds was quick to point out another reason we have to address the issue. He made it clear that we can't go to war without women anymore. He reminded those testifying and those watching the proceedings that women are an integral part of our present-day military. In fact, the pressure to recruit more of them has been on for a while. Not only do they help increase the size of our total forces, but they bring some unique and necessary skills with them. They are valued for intelligence gathering in places men can't typically go. They play a vital role when dealing with other women in countries where cultural practices prohibit interaction with men other than close family members. In certain parts of the world, these female troops are the only ones who can enter women's quarters during in-home inspections, the only ones who can talk to them about what their fathers, husbands, and sons are doing, and certainly the only ones who can search their person for hidden weapons.

And while there are these differences, women soldiers have

proven that they can effectively do what their male counterparts can do too. They provide border security, accompany convoys, drive trucks and tanks, fly aircraft, operate drones, and fire mortar rounds. As a woman, I also know that these ladies are great at multitasking under pressure. I think women are just hardwired that way. It's a skill we require for motherhood but it's put to good use in other areas too.

These days, women who qualify can even serve in elite Special Forces. And in May 2017 women also became eligible to serve in combat roles. During a historic graduation ceremony held at Fort Benning, in Georgia, eighteen enlisted women became our nation's first female infantrymen. I happened to be on the amphibious assault ship USS *Kearsarge* to commemorate Memorial Day with some of our service members when the news about how well these women did on their final tests spread to members of the other military branches. Words cannot describe the shared elation and pride I witnessed in everyone around me, but especially among the other women in the Marines and Navy. The importance of this milestone was felt most by them. Women used to be safeguarded from the dangers of the front lines, but as we fight in more insurgent-driven conflicts, the concept of a front line no longer exists. Danger surrounds you everywhere. In this way, female troops have already been engaged in active combat for quite some time. We are only acknowledging their proven ability to withstand that pressure now.

It was a relief to me that Congress recognized the importance of women in our armed forces, while also moving rapidly to deal legislatively with the issue of sexual harassment at hand. Just days after that momentous graduation ceremony at Fort Benning, Congress unanimously passed a bill that bans the sharing of nonconsensual nude photos throughout the US military. It was Congresswoman Martha McSally of my home state of Arizona who sponsored the Protecting the Rights of IndiViduals Against Technological Exploitation Act, otherwise known as the PRI-VATE Act. So many of us military families, and the public in general, are grateful that she did. It's an indication that we are, in fact, dealing head-on with some of our military's most perplexing demons in a timely and decisive manner. But it still gnaws at me that a bill was even necessary—that the acts against these women occurred at all, and that common decency has to be mandated rather than just expected of the people fighting to the right or left of you. Succeeding in life as well as in war means unconditionally respecting those taking up the cause with you.

While writing this book, I reached out to Congresswoman McSally for a broader perspective on the inclusion and treatment of female troops in the service. She is uniquely qualified to speak to this issue as she not only introduced the PRIVATE Act, she was also one of the first women in the United States Air Force to become a fighter pilot, the first woman in US history to fly a fighter aircraft into combat, and the first woman to command a combat aviation squadron.

I wanted to get a sense of the history of women in the Air Force, so I asked if she knew anything about what the first class of women who attended encountered. She was not there then, but she did say, "I have tremendous respect for them to be the first, to be the pioneers, to show up when the institution and the attitudes were not necessarily welcoming." Then she proceeded to tell me a story, which reflected the bravado of that time. Apparently when the last all-male class graduated in 1979 they had their motto em-blazoned on practically everything related to their class including their rings. It read: LCWB. I paused for a moment to try to figure out what the acronym stood for when she told me it meant "Last Class with Balls." They wanted to be sure to mark the changing times in a way no one would forget.

Things were somewhat different by the time she enrolled as part of the ninth class to include women at the Academy. Every grade before hers—the sophomores, juniors, and seniors—all had some gender diversity, so everyone had enough experience for the presence of women to be the *new normal*.

But that still didn't make it easy for the men to embrace the idea of female service members becoming anything more than cargo pilots or civilian aviators. There was still a law on the books that prohibited women from becoming fighter pilots, bomber pilots, or attack pilots. Her reaction to this news was classic. She thought, *What do you mean? I'm going through the same training as all of you. Just because I have ovaries you're telling me I can't fly that airplane?* That's when she resolved to be the first woman on the front lines as a combat pilot.

I found it interesting that she went on to describe her time at the academy as a very isolating experience—not just one that distanced the women from the men but one that distanced the women from each other too. It was as if those who did successfully assimilate were saying, "I'm one of the guys and you're not." She has since observed a similar phenomenon in civilian life among mixed groups of firefighters, police officers, and engineers. "Women in these situations, where they are the minority, can be more critical of each other," she explained. "Because if you're not stepping up and performing, or you're acting in a way that undermines us when I'm over here trying to prove that women belong, you're making me look bad."

She talked too about an air of paternalism on the part of some male supervisors and commanders. She explained that it creates a double standard that can easily cause divisions between men and women. She said, "It may not even be on purpose or it may not even be conscious, but sometimes you can have a male leader who is being easier on female subordinates because they almost look at them like daughters. They might say, 'Okay everybody, we're packing the pallets up to leave. The guys are going to do that and the girls are going to stay here and do the paperwork.' Without even realizing what they're doing, these male leaders are protecting the women. This commander just pissed off some of the guys because now they have to go out in the hot sun while the girls take it easy indoors. Because of this paternalistic approach, these male leaders inadvertently sow seeds of resentment within their team."

Congresswoman McSally also illustrated how this protectionism plays out among one's male peers, not just among male leadership. She said that male troops would often argue, "You women can't be fighter pilots because you might be shot down or you might become prisoners of war." They made it clear that they would "freak out if a woman was at risk of being captured or being sexually assaulted." Whenever male troops spoke in a hypothetical sense they would say, "We'd be so distracted trying to protect you; we wouldn't be able to do our jobs." Her reply to that was always, "Look, I appreciate your upbringing. I'm not trying to dismiss how you feel. But the reality is we go off to battle with each other after we've been through the same training." She would add, "If your male wingman got shot down and you didn't have that same deep horrible feeling in your heart—that same drive to do whatever it takes to get them home alive—then you are devaluing the life of your male teammates. Or if they make the ultimate sacrifice and you don't have the same tear in your eye when his body bag comes home as you would if it were a woman in that body bag, then you need to figure out how to wrap your head around that." Her final word on the subject was always, "You have to handle it. This is *your* problem. This isn't my problem. My problem is I'm going into battle with you trained and ready, capable and qualified. I earned this and now I'm on your team, so you are going to have to manage that in your mind. But whatever you do, don't devalue our male teammates by somehow insinuating that my life is more valuable than theirs, because it's not."

This little bit of history she provided certainly made the challenges the military has had to tackle clearer to me. Listening to the congresswoman talk about how isolated these women feel from each other at times made me wonder if this is one of the reasons why sexual harassment is so underreported. Our female troops may not always have other female confidants to turn to for support or for the encouragement to speak up. I saw how paternalism contributes to resentment too. And laced in the fears of what might happen to female pilots who were captured by the enemy is a deeply rooted objectification of women. It seemed to me as if they are often viewed as women first and capable soldiers second.

Congresswoman McSally is an impassioned speaker in general, but it was particularly evident when we moved on to the subject of the nude photo scandal. She described the situation as infuriating and demeaning to everyone. She explained, "It is infuriating because of what it does to the victims. It's infuriating because of what it does to the core of our fighting force too, which is the honor, the integrity, the camaraderie, the trust, the good order, the discipline, and esprit de corps—all the things that are underlying what has each of us fighting alongside each other, for each other, and for the country. When you start attacking each other, it's cancerous. The enemy is out there; the enemy isn't each other." She added, "It was disgusting, insulting, and inappropriate. And those are just the G-rated words that I'll give you."

She also found what it said about the perpetrators infuriating: "That they think they can just hide behind a computer and act that way because no one is looking or can identify them. That they can denigrate their fellow soldiers, denigrate their teammate—another person who wears the uniform, another person who trusts that your lives are in each other's hands. That they put the uniform on and come into work, walk past the military's core values posted in the hallway, and think that they actually embody them. That it's okay to be living this way. That they think that's not incongruent is deeply disturbing to me."

With regard to the PRIVATE Act, she acknowledged that it will require more than legislation. "This is a cultural issue and it's an *individual* issue," she explained. "It will take *everyone* choosing to embody these values, even when the stakes don't seem high to them and even when it may seem unpopular or uncool. It will take *everyone* refusing to be a bystander and certainly *everyone* refusing to be a denigrator." She added, "These seeds need to be planted and cultivated in *all* of our troops. We need to do our part in the military to reinforce these ideals, but ultimately these are character issues and you can't train character per se. So we've got to root out the perpetrators, hold them accountable, address the underlying culture, and make sure that we are recruiting and promoting and retaining individuals who live and act with the integrity that military life demands, because we just cannot have this kind of behavior."

If that seems like an incredibly tall order, I must tell you that the commitment and determination in her voice made it seem more possible than not. I am greatly encouraged by the fact that she and several other women who have served in our armed forces are now also serving in our legislative bodies throughout the nation. I do believe that they can help make her vision possible— that they can help make the military more inviting and respectful of all of the enormously capable women out there who have so much to offer.

There was something else Congresswoman McSally said before the conversation ended that provided further hope. She mentioned that since her days in the Air Force, she has studied the works of sociologists and other experts on the dynamics of minority groups. She explained, "According to these experts, when a minority group comprises less than twenty-five percent of the total population, they tend to be considered 'the other.' There are those that are 'alike' and those that are 'not alike.' An 'us' group and an 'other' group. But as soon as your group reaches or exceeds twenty-five percent of the population, you hit a kind of a tipping point where you're seen as an integrated part of the group—a critical part that can actually impact the behavior and dynamic of that group."

If this is true, then it would seem as if increasing the number of women in the US military might actually raise the prospects of serious change for the better. Presently, women comprise only 14.5 percent of the US military's population, but in time, if the trend toward higher female recruitment efforts continues, the culture holds the very real potential of evolving through greater peer interaction.

This idea is so intriguing to me that I think it might be worthwhile to look at the practices of our allies where women are already such an extensive part of the military. In Israel, for example, nearly one third of the international defense force is comprised of women. Every eligible citizen is obligated to serve despite gender. Whereas our society struggles with whether or not we want to make all Americans learn English, theirs accepts that at some point everyone of a certain age and eligibility will have to load, lock, and carry as part of their duty to country. These female soldiers are well integrated into a wide variety of operations just as American women are, though there are still some areas where they're prohibited, including the kinds of close combat and special occupations the United States has opened up recently to our female troops.

In Norway, women have been prevalent in the military for a long time too. Some have served as defense ministers, submarine commanders, and fighter jet pilots. But for the last four decades, unlike the Israeli military, female participation in Norway's armed forces was completely voluntary. It only became compulsory for women to serve in 2016. I'm sure that in advance of the change, their commanders carefully considered all the related issues. Now female troops there are trained and even housed in unisex barracks. The theory is that by routinely integrating men and women, a brother-sister bond will form—one that would be hard to violate as the troops work more closely together and rely on each other to survive. According to news reports from StraitsTimes.com and the BBC, it seems to be working.

But Norway appears to be testing out other theories at the same time. They recently implemented an all-female Special Forces training unit called the Jegertroppen (the Hunter Troop). Since this is the first of its kind in the world, I'm sure that many people in armed forces around the globe and certainly here at home will be keeping an eye on its results. It will be very interesting to watch developments of both practices closely, comparing and contrasting what works and why. There are close to forty countries where women participate in the military—whether they volunteer or are conscripted—so the opportunity to explore best practices is ripe.

These are interesting times for women, but I think they are for men too, as both have much to learn from each other. America has a hard-earned reputation for military ingenuity and we certainly love to win. We are also practiced at identifying demons and observing them closely enough to develop successful strategies for overcoming them, so I am optimistic that we will figure out a way to show greater respect for our female forces and also utilize them as the crucial military asset we know them to be.

Again, while my profession engages me in addressing these kinds of concerns publicly, I write about them here because these issues are important to me personally. Ask most brats where they grew up and they won't name a hometown, city, or state; they will tell you they grew up in the military. That's our home. So keeping a watchful eye on the issues they are grappling with is the same, in my mind, as keeping a watchful eye on family.

YOUR TURN

It is obviously embarrassing to have your demons pointed out to you by someone else, but if that happens to you as it did to me, take heart. Even try to be grateful for it. It is much better to know about your flaws than to continue on blindly. Having your attentions drawn to them provides you with an opportunity to correct them. It would be awful if my former news director never said a word to me about my being tardy all the time. Even if I was always prompt for the news, being late for everything else could have made my employers doubt just how much responsibility I could handle. If I hadn't broken that habit, I might not have been afforded the opportunity to cohost or anchor as many shows as I do today. I also believe the repercussions would have spread beyond my career, especially as my life expanded to include so many others who rely on me daily, including my husband and children. Because someone cared enough to tell me, I made changes in my behavior that I am grateful for to this day.

To Deal with Your Demons you will need to:

- Make a list of every habit you have even if no one has pointed it out to you before. Drill instructors have a laserlike ability to home in on areas that need work. You will need to adopt that same kind of focus for this first step.
- Look at each habit one at a time and write down all the ways it helps you and all of the ways it hinders you. Give extra thought to how it is impacting your goals and the people around you. You will instantly know where on the scale from harmless to detrimental this habit falls.
- Observe your environment and note any circumstances that trigger the habit.
- Ask yourself if there is a way to avoid or minimize that trigger.
- Devise a plan for overcoming this habit by exploring the most successful ways others have overcome it before you.

- Recruit one of your special forces to help you stay on plan. You may want to write them a note with specifics about how they should do this so they don't become overbearing and you don't resent them for their genuine efforts to be supportive.
- Keep a journal or mark your calendar every day, noting how you did so you can monitor your progress.
- Some experts suggest that you stick vigilantly to your objective for sixty-six consecutive days to help permanently break your habit. They believe that this is how long it takes to affect lasting change.

Note that once you have rid yourself of your unwanted habits, you can improve your life and your prospects for achieving success by adapting the above process to introduce new, healthier, more constructive habits in place of the old ones. Again, this is what boot camp does so well—it swaps out all the behaviors that impede success and teaches young recruits all the ones that will enable them to survive and thrive.

Also note you don't have to wait for an unwanted habit to develop. You can be preemptive about it. In other words, you can bar a bad habit from ever entering your world at all. We can all look around and see people slacking off, overeating, drinking too much, worrying all the time, or facing any number of other common challenges. Be mindful of those tendencies. We are all predisposed to them under the wrong circumstances, so seriously try to control them before they ever get a chance to possess you.

Hopefully the flaws you discover in yourself after taking a closer look will prove to be relatively minor. But should they pose more of a challenge than you might have expected, I encourage you to take a cue from my father's generation of war heroes. If one of your demons feels too big for you to handle on your own, know that our culture offers so many more ways to help you now than it ever did before. And those ways no longer carry a stigma. So don't be afraid to seek a trained professional's guidance. Whether you wish to overcome depression, anxiety, or addiction, or you wish to lose weight, exercise more effectively, unclutter your environment, become more organized at home or at work, curb the amount of time you spend on social media, or be more prudent with your money, there are people with skills who can help. This book is all about enabling you to be the best you can be. Reaching out for guidance from someone who has an expertise in an area that you don't is actually a very good habit to acquire.

Rule #3

STAY READY

When you are a pilot in the military you never know when the call for help will come. It's not as if troops in distress schedule appointments for pickup in advance. If they contact you for your assistance, you must be prepared to be en route in seconds. It takes a very special type of training to have that kind of response time. You have to be physically agile, mentally alert, and emotionally prepared for any eventuality. All three aspects of your being have to align for you to be able to calmly and capably handle the challenge ahead of you.

There was a time during my father's second tour of duty in Vietnam when several planes were downed in this one hot spot west of Da Nang, just on the border of Laos. Everyone was concerned about it. They didn't want to lose valuable aircraft, and they certainly didn't want to lose lives. My father was very fond of all the men in his unit. He often spoke about their skills. Some of the younger ones could make a plane spin on its tail. They'd compete to do all kinds of fancy maneuvers. When word came in one evening that a pilot who crashed in that hot spot needed rescuing, my dad headed out as part of the retrieval team. It was a dangerous mission and everyone was aware of that. Three flare pots burning in the darkness guided the team to the stranded pilot's location, but they still had to clear a rough tree line in heavy winds in order to successfully pull the young aviator and the remains of the plane out. Somehow they managed. My dad explained that when you are close the way all the men in his unit were, you are motivated by that bond and you just get in there and do what you have to do without fear. He told me that he had an epiphany later that night. "I realized just how much we pilots were each other's Gods in every challenge we faced," he said. "It was miraculous what we were able to do for each other at times."

It is apparent from this story that our troops need equal parts physical and mental strength to pull off a rescue like that. It's also evident that they need a little faith too—faith in themselves, each other, their training, and sometimes in a force larger than them.

My dad, as you know, was taught to fly and maintain aircraft by the Army branch of the military. It was a highly specialized training, unique for the time and the war the United States was fighting back then.

The physical component to being a pilot is extremely important. The stress that flying an aircraft puts on the body cannot be underestimated, whether operating an attack helicopter, a transport plane, or a gunship. Add to that what was required once a pilot like my dad landed—everything from loading and unloading heavy munitions to trekking through rough terrains, scaling signal towers to make repairs, moving quickly to install communications equipment in the field, or carrying injured soldiers—and you understand why improving endurance, strength, flexibility, and mobility is so important.

To get a better sense of how pilots train to get ready today, it might be helpful to look at how the Air Force currently gets its members in optimal shape. Their training and the duties they perform are somewhat different from what my dad went through, but also wide-ranging and physically challenging. The process begins with boot camp. Passing the physical performance test at the end is key. A recruit's final scores indicate his or her overall strength, stamina, and cardio-respiratory fitness. To pass this test you have to complete a targeted number of push-ups within one minute and a targeted number of sit-ups within one minute followed by a one-and-a-half-mile run and a two-mile run timed at the designated speed for your gender. Depending on the recruit's level of performance, pull-ups may be added to the test as well.

Meeting the minimum graduation standard, which is tough by any measure, will land one in the Liberator category. Some recruits who do even better than that rise to either Thunderbolt level, or to the ultimate Warhawk status. I don't know how many of you reading this book can do between forty-five and seventy-five push-ups, between fifty and eighty sit-ups, run a mile and a half between 8:08 and 11:57 minutes or two miles between 13:30 and 16:45 minutes. I have so much respect for the determination and commitment it takes to do this.

Every recruit also goes through weapons training, learns various combat and survival techniques, and engages in practical field simulations too. There's rarely a time when recruits aren't in physical motion, running or carrying out repetitive tasks or maneuvers until they are completed to satisfaction. This repetition is important no matter which branch of the military you are training for. The brilliance behind these drills is that while troops are building new skills and growing stronger every day, they are also developing *muscle memory*. That's the training my dad always talked to me about when I was younger. You can be an expert marksman when it's just you and the practice target at the shooting range—in other words, when there are no external pressures bearing down on you. But performing to that same degree of excellence when you are under extreme duress could never happen without constant practice and deeply ingrained muscle memory. He explained that panic acts like mental exhaustion. When you are really anxious and stressed out, as you would be in a live combat situation, your brain gets clouded. It's actually muscle memory that triggers the mind to do by rote whatever it is that has to get done. Your physical test scores have to be really solid during basic training because it's those abilities that support your mental acuity when it's required. Essentially, the muscle memory that's built up in training is what helps soldiers multitask even when they are totally exhausted.

Believe it or not, this is just the bare minimum training some of our Air Force recruits will go through. The physical demands increase when some seek to become pararescuemen (also called parajumpers), combat control technicians, or special operations weather technicians.

The parajumpers are trained to rescue troops that are stranded, injured, or in any other type of distress, while the combat control technicians are trained to serve as air traffic controllers, monitoring and directing the arrival and departure of all aircraft and ensuring the overall safety of the airspace. They are also tasked with going behind enemy lines to set up drop zones and airfields, in the same way my dad did, before any of the other troops arrive. The special ops weather technicians are, of course, incredibly skilled meteorologists.

To fulfill these roles, it's not enough for them to learn how to function and survive in the air; they must also be able to function and survive *wherever they land*, no matter what the geographic or climate conditions are.

And that's not all. The mental requirements get tougher too. All of these troops will go on to attend Army Airborne; Army Combat Divers; Army Parachutist; and Air Force Survival, Evasion, Resistance, and Escape schools, as well as Navy Underwater Egress training. Depending upon their specialty, there is even more specific training on top of that.

In the process, these pilots are also developing more subtle qualities. All of this military training reinforces a respect for tradition. It's staggering to think about how these exercises have served countless other soldiers in past wars and conflicts. By extension, this hard work makes troops believe in the historical strength of our country. The United States has proven time and again that it is not going to settle for a mediocre military. When soldiers recognize how far they and their peers have come because of their instruction, they also recognize that America's military is built on the expectation of excellence. These are all important mentally and emotionally fortifying aspects of the conditioning.

Another great facet of the training is that it helps troops *know their purpose*. And knowing their purpose gives them a sense of belonging. It teaches them to act in unison. From there, it is a short step to embracing a *one for all and all for one* spirit so necessary for group success—the kind that drove my father and the other pilots in his unit to be each other's miracle workers in times of distress.

The more you think about the demands placed on these troops, the more you realize that they can only reach such a high level of performance if their mind, body, and spirit are working together.

ON MORE THAN A WING AND A PRAYER

The military cultivates its servicemen and -women to this degree so they aren't in the thick of war when they first realize the many different kinds of human strength they have to summon in order to survive. Even the most intense crash courses are no match for the cumulative power you build up when you maintain ongoing, dedicated, and disciplined training in these three pivotal areas of personal development.

The concept behind "Stay Ready" applies to civilian life as well. We all need to be able to rely on ourselves, and we must be ready for those who rely on us too. We have to develop a regimen that keeps us physically, mentally, and emotionally resilient if we are going to be fit enough to face life's many challenges. We also have to practice that regimen even when things are going well.

FIGHT OR FLIGHT

I was fortunate to be raised with a strong foundation in all three areas of personal development. I was surrounded by the example of troops engaged in physical and mental training while living on base. Both of my parents valued exercise and healthy eating habits and instilled them in me as well. I enjoyed school, studied hard, and had interests in many different subjects. Being surrounded by so many interesting people and living in so many different places also expanded my mind. And my family had a deep spiritual practice. We attended services every week at a local church so we could connect and spend quality time in worship and in community with our civilian neighbors. We tried to remain hopeful in tough times and relied on prayer especially when my father was deployed and we had concerns for his safety.

When I first devised the rule "Stay Ready," I thought of it as making an appointment with your dreams. It meant that by preparing for something with diligence and commitment, you were showing yourself and others how much you believed you could accomplish those dreams.

It still means that; however, the rule's meaning expanded for me when I was anchoring the evening news on weeknights in Kansas City. It was an exciting time in my career. But as often is the case, the good times were coupled with tough times. As I mentioned earlier, I was being stalked by a former boyfriend and coworker. He had terrorized me for more than two years. The incidents began with obsessive phone calls and escalated to having my car keyed with sexually explicit words. This stalker eventually broke into my apartment, which only had one way out. He blocked that exit and a violent struggle ensued. Neighbors on multiple floors could hear me screaming for help. The police arrived and I survived. Somehow, I mustered all the strength I needed in the moment and was fortunate that others came to my aid as well. However, it was not the last time that he would break into my home, even after I moved.

The Kansas City (KCMO) police department subsequently placed officers outside my building and the local TV station where I worked. The court system in Jackson County, Missouri, saw me on many occasions seeking orders of protection and filing complaints against the stalker. Yet, he persisted. The Prosecutor's Office, led by Claire McCaskill, who was then a prominent local attorney and is now a prominent US senator, assigned my case to be heard in an effort to stop this madman from continuing to invade my life.

During one of the fact-and-evidence-gathering interviews with the District Attorney's Office about what was happening to me, we closely reviewed the stalker's actions. The DA's Office noticed a pattern: This guy had a huge jump on police and everyone else because he knew me so well. He was aware of my routine, eating habits, friends, and coworkers. He even knew my weaknesses. The stalking case was filed as a domestic case because we had dated in another city. Our former relationship left him armed with all sorts of information that aided his ability to terrorize me. When he crossed several state lines—expressly moving from North Carolina to Missouri to come after me—his sudden appearance meant that he had the element of surprise working in his favor too.

Looking at this profile and modus operandi, the DA's Office told me that all of this allowed him to "stay ready" for any opportunity to wreak havoc in my life and in the lives of those around me.

I was the target of this man's mission: If he could not have me, then no one else would either. His preparedness clearly played a huge part in how he executed his mission.

I decided to fight back against any fears or future threats by learning from his example. I upgraded my readiness. To do this, I leaned on the amazing local officers of the KCMO police department. They are not military, but they are a fighting force of sorts. I took a cue from their preparedness and learned to fire a weapon, took self-defense courses, and kept a log of every time I was followed or contacted by the stalker. And when things got particularly bad, I worked closely with a private detective so that I could learn the stalker's patterns the way he had learned mine.

After spending time in and out of county jail, and after facing a high-profile trial covered by the local media, this stalker got what was coming to him and I finally saw justice meted out. That is when I extended this rule to mean: *Stay ready so you don't have to get ready.*

Oddly, the stalker's dangerous pursuit of me had been so efficient that it became both a lesson and a motivation for me to be strong in as many ways as I possibly could.

READY AND ABLE

After that ordeal, I designed a regimen to help me stay ready for whatever might help me *fulfill my dreams* and for whatever might arise unexpectedly to *challenge those dreams*. I contemplated again how the military conditions the body, mind, and spirit to be prepared for anything and I adapted this three-tiered approach to my own goals. I knew all about the training the troops went through to make themselves alert, responsive, and resilient. I wanted to accomplish the same outcome with activities that were feasible for my lifestyle. My thinking was that I'd be more likely to stick to the conditioning if the regimen included activities I already liked and engaged in from time to time. That's why the regimen I developed and still use today involves running, yoga, and prayer.

These are three practices I had relied on separately for body, mind, and spirit strengthening at earlier times in my life. But now I was consciously making an effort to do all three consistently in my life. The plan was and still is to *stay ready*. I practice all three to this day. Each is important for different reasons.

Hitting the Ground Running

In an almost Forrest Gump–like fashion, running suddenly became a staple activity for me during my freshman year in college. University of California, Santa Barbara (UCSB), is known for its majestic mountains that seem to custom-frame the beautiful Pacific Coast, so it was an inviting place to start.

That first year was stressful. It constantly challenged the young girl in me to step into womanhood, responsibility, and a new level of accountability for my actions and decisions. No more Mom and Dad to help me navigate situations on a daily basis. Of course, they were there for the big stuff, but now I was on my own to figure most things out by myself.

At first, my route began as a simple loop outside of San Nicolas, my dormitory building. It was a short jaunt from the lagoon situated next to the dorm to a bike path that I followed around the west side of campus. The whole run didn't take more than thirty minutes to complete at a pace my now eleven-year-old daughter would consider slow! But it allowed me time to clear my head and to embrace my new role as an adult. I had worked summer jobs, traveled with my family on vacations, and certainly relocated to different bases and military towns before, but getting used to this new environment was different. I experienced an "aloneness" I hadn't known before, which required discipline and focus to combat. I thought back to how my dad's tennis matches with friends helped him stay centered after he retired from the Army and changes in his personal life occurred too. While I love tennis, activities involving other people seemed out of reach for me at the time. It was too early in my development of friendships on campus. So I began to jog.

That initial thirty minutes on the bike path quickly evolved into ninety minutes. I was covering miles now—and at a faster pace. I was *running*. If you choose to pursue a cardiovascular workout too, try to persist. I understand why the best runners say no postponements, cancellations, or excuses allowed. You will see a marked improvement if you stick with it. The people at Nike are right: "Just do it."

What I also love about running is that it doesn't require much: Just me, a good pair of shoes, and time. At UCSB I ran in the rain. I ran in heat so dry I had to hydrate just to sweat. I ran when things were going well at school and when things weren't. The sounds of nature and my own breathing as I tackled the uneven ground on nearby hiking trails and the mountainside became my friends. Before long I was running half marathons in Santa Barbara and neighboring communities.

My first full marathon didn't come until years later. When I got a post-college job working as a temp for a legal firm, those same stressors I felt at UCSB during my freshman year instantly returned. But this time, I realized that I was more than ready to assume the autonomy, responsibility, and accountability my new environment demanded (especially because I was being paid for it!). I was also ready to train for races—10Ks, half marathons, and yes, once a year for a while I ran the Los Angeles Marathon.

Because staying in that peak condition takes time, I tend to speed walk the longer races for charity these days. In September 2015, when my aunt Mary was diagnosed with breast cancer, I entered the AVON 39. It was a long challenge consisting of 26.2 miles on day one and 13.1 on day two, but I persevered.

What I find amazing about this particular exercise—especially if you do it in a city like New York—is that it not only benefits you aerobically, it also helps you develop the ability to hold two or more thoughts in your head at once. Although it can appear as if we runners are tuning out the world when we're in the zone, we are actually operating on several levels simultaneously. We're listening to feedback from our body about how hard we are pushing it and we're also paying keen attention to everything else around us including curbs, potholes, dog-walkers, pedestrians, delivery trucks, buses, cars, and of course the bicyclist that always seems to come out of nowhere. In fact, if we're not that attuned to the world around us, what we're really running is the risk of getting seriously hurt. In my experience, this sport not only provides good fitness training, it helps you practice and perfect your multi-tasking skills, which in turn gives you the confidence to overcome whatever challenges you face. I find it to be the perfect sport for my mission to Stay Ready.

In fact, the more I run, the more I realize the military is right: There is a very strong mind-body connection at work when you are physically active. The idea that repetitive exercise develops a kind of shorthand with the brain that enables the mind to function automatically even under stress makes more and more sense to me, not just as I become an increasingly proficient runner, but as I also read about the subject. There are a number of scientific studies in the area of neurogenesis and neuroplasticity that support the notion that physical exercise has a positive impact on our cognitive abilities and performance. For instance, researchers at the National Institute on Aging in the United States have found that exercised muscles generate a protein called cathepsin B, which triggers baby neurons to form in the hippocampus of the brain. Other researchers have also found that when you exercise, the blood flow triggers new pathways to form between neurons.

Is it possible that those new pathways are speeding up the conversations between the mind and body to improve the quality and nature of both our physical and mental response times? I guess you will just have to keep active to find out.

Striking a Pose

Yoga is another wonderful practice to help me stay ready for both opportunities and challenges. One of its many benefits is that it teaches you how to slow your heart rate and empty your mind enough to be able to take in new material. The deep and controlled breathing that is so integral to yoga is what induces this calm state and is also what enables you to be more perceptive and rational when you apply the same type of breathing to difficult situations in the world outside of the gym or yoga studio. How often have you been told to just breathe deeply when you've been nervous or tense? It's a technique that is universally believed to help keep you relaxed and focused.

There are other ways to condition yourself to breathe deeper and to use that practice to remain calm under pressure as well— Pilates and tai chi both come to mind. What also comes to mind is a sedentary alternative my parents have used to excellent effect for years. It's the practice of *sitting still*. Those who live in the southern regions of the United States do it all the time when they porch sit. I'd go so far as to say that Southerners have raised sitting still to an art form. While it sounds so *country*, I think city dwellers should try it sometimes too. Every home my family lived in while I was growing up had a screened-in porch for this purpose and if the house didn't come with one, then my father built a porch himself. He and my mother would sit outside for hours taking in the silence. I remember begging them to turn on some music or to play a board game with me because in my restless youth I just couldn't stand being idle like that for so long. But those respites from all the bustle and noise definitely served a purpose. Both of my parents were heart-stoppingly relaxed. And though I protested it then, I recognize now how necessary it is to have stillness in your life.

So much vies for our attention in the quick-paced world we live in that we all need to carve out some time for peace and quiet at least once daily. I cannot have electronic devices constantly buzzing around me at all times. As someone who works six days a week, I especially look forward to having a calm home on weekends. Your brain needs to regenerate, and while sleep provides you with rest, sitting still can repair the frayed edges and reconnect you to the things that tend to get pushed aside by more immediate demands.

The key to sitting still is just letting thoughts wash over you. There is no need to act on them in the moment. Just recognizing them is enough. Saying to yourself, "Yeah, okay I see that. I'm not going to address it right now. I'm just going to acknowledge that it's there," is really all you have to do.

Because constant interruptions tend to scatter thoughts, I truly believe that silence is necessary to take in the goodness and blessings that are coming to you.

By the way, if you're skeptical about the power of sitting still the way I once was, there are studies to reassure you of this as well. According to the scientific journal *Brain Structure & Function*, scientists found that two hours of sitting in silence a day leads to the production of new neurons in the brain too. These scientists hail from the Center for Regenerative Therapies in Dresden, Germany, where they are making many more exciting discoveries related to neurogenesis. Once I read about their findings I knew for sure that both of my parents were right about porch sitting. If time spent relaxing—including sitting in silence and/or doing yoga—can make you more mentally agile and alert, then it is definitely time well spent.

I never saw my dad do downward-facing dog, and he certainly didn't have porch-sitting opportunities while he was deployed— that's for sure. But he did say that the military cultivates the discipline of stillness in its troops for its own reasons and in its own way.

"In battle you cannot be in constant motion because when you are, it's impossible to hear the enemies' footsteps," he explained. "For this reason, soldiers are trained to relax in battle, to really take in the moment, to make sure that they are focused on executing the plan they've constructed in order to succeed. You simply cannot do that with a cacophony of dialogue and movement going on at the same time."

A commander may not use yoga per se, but what he is really teaching his unit is the same skill: A way to be at peace while indefinitely waiting—a way to maintain supernatural patience. These are common principles of both yoga and meditative prayer and they are also traits in some of the most effective and responsive soldiers. It was clear to me after my father returned from

Vietnam that he brought the benefits of both his physical and
stillness training home with him. The techniques and lessons he
learned in the Army helped reduce his stress levels and gave him
greater clarity of mind. I don't think I ever saw him get riled
about anything. Even at age eighty, he still maintains a wonder-
fully calm demeanor.

Keeping the Faith

Prayer, the third component in my regimen, can take the form
of focused meditation, reading spiritual text and literature, or
communing with nature. It can be whatever it means to you.

Although it is different from the other two components—even
from sitting still—I find that it sometimes follows one or both of
the other activities, which is why I believe they go hand in hand. If
I've gone running, for instance, and I'm just sitting still afterward
or I've done some yoga and have ended in my favorite position,
Savasana—where I am basically lying down with my eyes closed,
thinking about nothing in particular, letting the ground catch my
weight and just feeling open—I will often say a prayer. It could
be as simple as a word or two of gratitude, or now that I have
ordered my thoughts, it can be a concise request for assistance in
some matter. Then I wait quietly a little while longer before I get
up and go about the rest of my day. Strong faith teaches you that
when you do all of the talking, there's no way God can help you,
because you're not listening. So I try to create moments when
He can really speak to me and I am prepared to hear Him.

Yes, there is proof that prayer impacts the brain too. Dr. An-
drew Newberg, from the Thomas Jefferson University Hospital
in Philadelphia, Pennsylvania, has conducted decades' worth of

research and is a prolific author on the subject. What his studies reveal is that brain chemistry changes when we pray for an extended period of time. One of the most significant changes occurs in the part of the brain associated with the self. Whether he was studying the brain patterns of Buddhist monks, Sufi mystics, or Franciscan nuns engaged in meditative prayer, he noticed that this part of the brain began shutting down. The same result occurred when he observed a Methodist minister engaged in intercessory prayer—a type of prayer that focuses on the needs of others.

As interesting as the suppressed awareness of self is, it is not proof that the subjects in these studies are actually connecting with God or becoming more at one with the Universe while praying. What can be confirmed, however, is that as these neural pathways become less active, others are becoming more developed. As Dr. Newberg explains it, "The more you focus on something, whether that's math or auto racing or football or God—the more that becomes your reality—the more it becomes written into the neural connections of your brain."

It could be said that for many people, prayer is a statement of intention. Putting a wish before God or out into the Universe is a way of focusing on that desired goal. Seeking help from a higher power in achieving that wish indicates its importance to you. It may just be that once your intention is inscribed into your neural pathways you are more likely to find ways to help that desire come to fruition. Or it may be that another powerful being is listening and helping too. Either way, it seems as if prayer could be a very useful tool for us when we want to gather all the help we can get from ourselves or from outside sources.

Of course, prayer is not a part of military training. As a government institution, the armed services must keep church and state separate so as to respect the many and varied beliefs of our troops, including the beliefs of atheists and agnostics. But what the military does provide is a strong sense of moral duty. This is most evident in each military branch's mottos. The Air Force's mantra, for example, "Integrity first. Service before self. Excellence in all we do," speaks to the larger good each member seeks to accomplish during their enlistment. In many ways, these mottos are the military's nondenominational creed. They represent shared core values and a belief in the ideals they are fighting for— most notably for democracy and the preservation of freedom. Oftentimes, the pep talks my dad and other leaders gave to their subordinates before battle reminded our troops of such purposes larger than themselves.

And though it wasn't often spoken about, I know there were times when my dad and many others found themselves privately calling upon their respective gods to watch over them because they felt a higher power was needed to protect them from danger or to help them win a tough battle. My father is not a particularly religious man, meaning his faith isn't heavily guided by the routines or traditions of an institution. But he is a spiritual man— one who knows that war can humble even the most highly skilled soldiers into calling for backup. There are some men and women in the Special Forces who might also refrain from talking about spirituality, but whom I suspect recognize that because they are often asked to do extrahuman things, they may sometimes need extrahuman help.

At the end of the day, I'm very glad I engage in running, yoga, and prayer on an ongoing basis. They do what I intended them to: They train the different parts of me—my mind, body, and spirit—to work in tandem toward achieving whatever my goal may be. I am also encouraged to know that there is some scientific study to support these ideas and that there is military precedent as well.

TAKE ON THE CHALLENGE

One thing that might help you customize your own practice for staying ready is to look around and see how other people do it. It probably won't surprise you to hear that those who are the most highly skilled at reacting on a dime to an opportunity *or* a challenge are military spouses and their children. No matter what is happening in their lives, they accept that disruption is always a possibility.

When I was speaking recently to military spouse Paola Harrell, a family friend and the widow of Major General Ernest James Harrell, she told me that *staying ready* for her often meant having the new quarters she just moved into fully primed for entertaining within two to three weeks of arrival. That included having the home completely furnished and decorated with pictures hanging up on the wall. It also meant being prepared to receive a call from her husband asking if he could bring a few of his officers home for a meal that same evening. She said she always had a standing rib roast, a ham, or a leg of lamb in the refrigerator waiting to be made. These were hungry lieutenants and captains she would be feeding. And if there were too many people for dinner, she had to be able to pull together enough for a cocktail party.

In many ways, the role Paola played cannot be underestimated. Because she stayed ready, what her husband and those other officers were able to discuss over a home-cooked meal or a glass of wine very likely helped them to stay ready in the field. She acknowledged that it was a special skill, but she told me that she also knew civilians who had to stay ready to meet similar demands. She had a neighbor who was an executive for JCPenney at the time who also had to move a lot and who entertained guests many times too. It was just something you had to do if you wanted to get ahead.

When I look around today at people with similar aspirations, I see them traveling and entertaining as well. I also see them participating in athletic activities that expressly challenge the body, mind, and spirit to the level some warriors do. Many male and female CEOs gravitate to competitions like the IRONMAN Triathlon precisely because they are physically, mentally, and emotionally rigorous challenges. *Forbes* magazine frequently features articles about industry titans who do this to test and prove their competencies across several disciplines. Participants have to have more than a goal. They have to have a vision and a strategy to achieve the desired results under extremely stressful conditions. It takes skillful planning, preparation, and execution—the same skills required in the boardroom. Practicing these skills in different settings assures that they will become second nature wherever and whenever they are applied. Engaging in these challenges is another way of staying ready.

Another popular challenge high-achievers are taking up to help condition themselves on multiple levels is The Murph Challenge. This is a test of mental and physical stamina named for Navy SEAL Lieutenant Michael Murphy, who lost his life while serving our country in 2005. He and three fellow SEALs were conducting a reconnaissance mission when they found themselves outnumbered by the Taliban on a steep and rocky mountainside in Afghanistan's Kunar Province. The team was drawing heavy fire from more than fifty anti-coalition militia positioned above them on higher ground. When Lieutenant Murphy sensed he was all out of options he stepped into the clearing long enough to call for a helicopter extraction. He knew leaving his cover was risky but he did it anyway in an effort to help save his peers. Sadly, gunner mate second class (SEAL) Danny Dietz and sonar technician second class (SEAL) Matthew Axelson perished with him, as did eight additional Navy SEALs and eight Nighthawk Army Stalkers who attempted their rescue. Only the fourth soldier on the mountainside with them that day, hospital corpsman second class (SEAL) Marcus Luttrell, lived to tell the story of his and the others' bravery.

Lieutenant Murphy's favorite CrossFit workout of the day included a one-mile run followed by one hundred pull-ups, two hundred push-ups, three hundred squats, and another one-mile run, all completed while wearing a twenty-pound vest (aka body armor). Since the lieutenant's death, many people have trained for and endeavored to complete this same physical challenge. It's actually become a Memorial Day tradition. Taking on The Murph Challenge not only raises your game, it also commemorates the life and valor of Lieutenant Murphy and other war heroes like him and raises much-needed money to provide scholarships to the children of fallen soldiers. Celebrities Chris Pratt and John Krasinski are just two of the well-known, highly accomplished people who have attempted and completed the challenge. The training no doubt helped them *stay ready* for their next demanding acting roles.

As it turns out, many military veterans participate in the IRONMAN and The Murph Challenge too. This type of training is familiar territory to them. They often miss the advanced level of physical achievement and purposefulness they had when they were in the armed services. These events reconnect them to both.

By the way, if you are already a physically active person and are looking to take your training to the next level, are contemplating joining the US military and want to train in advance, or are a vet who wants to maintain a regimen like the one you had kept while in the armed services, check out Military.com. It's one of the most comprehensive sites for those interested in all things military. Among its many features, it lists some of the best veteran-owned businesses established to help you get in optimal shape.

Bear in mind, though, that you don't have to train like a warrior or conquer the IRONMAN, The Murph Challenge, or Mount Everest tomorrow to stay ready. Maybe a combination of swimming, tai chi, and meditation would work well for you. The objective here is to find activities that strengthen the mind, body, and spirit, and the way the three work in sync to help you accomplish your goals. Start out at a level you feel comfortable with and push yourself beyond that stage one step at a time. Set realistic goals for yourself, and when you reach each interim goal, raise the bar a little higher until one day you realize you have far surpassed the maximum level you thought you could accomplish.

As I've said before, I do *not* have military-caliber training, so what I aimed to do when I first conceived *my regimen* was to find a way to help me become stronger in all the ways I believed I needed to be in order to succeed, especially when challenges to my success arose. The combination of running, yoga, and prayer was a great way for me to accomplish that goal.

What basic conditioning will you pursue? What further special-tactics training could put you over the top and help you achieve great things in your professional, personal, and communal life? Let's get specific right now.

A good first step if you are not someone who is presently active is to speak with your doctor, consult a trainer, visit your local fitness center, and/or do some additional online research to help you determine your overall fitness goals. Be sure to write those goals down and post them somewhere you are apt to see them. Reminding yourself to make good on your personal promises can really help.

Next, think about what might be your equivalent to running. As you try to key in on the best sport for you, think like a journalist and ask the *who, what, where, how,* and *why* questions. In other words:

For the *who* question, ask yourself: Are you someone who enjoys team sports? Someone who is more attracted to lone activities? Or are you someone who enjoys working out at a gym, having access to a trainer and perhaps to scheduled classes?

Sometimes a commitment to teammates is what keeps us regularly participating in an activity. They not only rely on us to be there, but they drive us to be better, to improve, to keep at it. It's very similar to the way the other members in a military unit drive their fellow soldiers to be their best.

Other times the flexibility of exercising whenever and wherever you want to is what helps us maintain our commitment.

It's okay too if you are someone who really likes to mix things up. There are people who golf, play tennis, and run because the first two allow them to exercise with different friends who like those same sports and the latter is an alternative for those times when no one else is around.

And because fitness centers with trainers are everywhere, their convenience makes them a great option to be considered as well. Sometimes we all need trainers to bring out the best in us, just as recruits need drill instructors to do the same for them.

Once you know who will inspire you best—a team, yourself, an instructor, or a mix of different players—you will have already made progress homing in on the right type of physical sport or activity for you.

To answer the *what* question: Think about all of the activities and sports you've enjoyed in the past. Reach as far back as grade school if you have to. The aim is to help you identify pursuits you really like, have fond memories of, and may already have a capacity for. Remember: If it is something you like doing, there is an increased likelihood that you will have the discipline to keep on doing it. What we are looking for is ongoing commitment.

The *where* and *how* questions demand that you investigate places or organizations where you can participate in your sport. Yes, fitness centers are everywhere. Paths for running and biking are everywhere, and depending upon where you live, trails for hiking are too. But if you are resuming your childhood passion for figure skating or jujitsu, you've got to know where to find the nearest rink or dojo and their hours. If basketball, football, or baseball is your thing, then check out where the nearest leagues and fields are. They've got to be accessible for you to stick with your goal, unless of course your passion for the sport will take you miles out of your way.

The *why* question centers on what core strengths—physical, mental, and emotional—you hope this sport will help you develop. The good news is that many sports work on all three levels. They condition you while also lifting mood and clearing brain fatigue.

Hopefully these questions will guide you to doing something you love as much as I love running. I've heard of people who swear by the cardiovascular benefits of salsa and make time to dance three to four times a week.

Once you choose a physical sport or activity, pursue it several times each week for a minimum of three weeks. Committing to this period of time will help you establish a habit. Re-up your commitment every three weeks until you no longer need to make that kind of contract with yourself because exercising has become an integral part of your life.

Now determine what your equivalent to yoga might be. Will you take up tai chi, qigong, walking, or cycling to clear your mind? Or will you try some form of sitting in silence too?

Record your scheduled quiet times and any important thoughts or ideas that came to you in a diary if you wish. When you see how helpful this practice is you will want to continue it. Again, pursue this for at least a half hour daily for three solid weeks to help an ongoing habit to form.

Lastly, what will be your equivalent to prayer? Meditation? Community service? Keeping a gratitude journal? Or maybe you prefer reading inspiring literature? Speaking or writing daily affirmations? Attending a house of worship? Practicing wonderment or, as some people call it, communing with nature? Stargazing, taking in the sunset or sunrise, walking along the beach, are all awe-inspiring experiences that lift the spirit. Did any intentions or insights come to you during your time of reflection? If so note them so you can remember to follow through on them.

Again, pursue these spiritual activities or conversations daily with yourself, your neural pathways, your guardian angels, your

God, the Universe, or whomever else you turn to for help fulfilling your most important goals. As with all the other suggestions,
maintain this practice consistently for three weeks to help a habit
of earnest dialogue to form.

I'm wagering that getting your mind, body, and spirit in good
enough shape to act in tandem with each other can help you accomplish three times whatever you had hoped to before reading
this book. Want to take that bet?

Rule #4

DEVISE YOUR MISSION

My father made many narrow escapes during his time in Vietnam. I described one earlier that occurred in Vũng Tàu, where an artilleryman fortunately came to his rescue. But there were other times when he was left strictly to his own devices. Occasions like the one I'm about to recount were the scariest.

He told me that he had just dropped off combat soldiers and ordnance near an outlying airfield where US ground troops were positioned. He was hoping for an uneventful return to camp along the Saigon River when he spied Vietcong snipers in the tall trees along the banks of the water. He was in an eight- or nine-cylinder Beaver with a radio engine, which for those of you unfamiliar with various kinds of military aircraft is a pretty conspicuous-sized plane under the circumstances. He knew going in that it wasn't exactly conducive to keeping a low profile but it was necessary to transport the heavy load of men and equipment he just delivered.

By the time he caught sight of the enemy he was already under heavy fire. All he could see was a blaze of gunshot heading
directly for his face. Although the snipers were armed with rifles,
they weren't just shooting bullets. They were shooting marker
rounds and those rounds were coming in red hot. They were literally on fire. Miraculously, not a single one hit him.

He was barely in the air at this point, since he had just left the
runway. He made a split-second decision, thinking his best option
was to continue at a low level across the river until he could climb
to a more viable altitude. But that, as it happened, was not the
best strategy. With his vision obscured by the barrage, he changed
course again, dunking the plane and following a tributary, which
luckily had no cables to block his advancement. When he was
sure he had passed danger, he guided the aircraft upward and
away. He could see the Vietcong scurrying for better placement
in the trees, but he was already gone by the time they were newly
positioned.

When he arrived safely back at the base and exited the plane,
his knees buckled and he fell to the ground. He hadn't been hit,
but the plane clearly had been. It was riddled with holes. The
crew on the strip rushed to get him to a flight surgeon for exam-
ination, but all he wanted to do was analyze what went wrong for
the next time.

One thing every Army pilot knows is that there is no such
thing as a routine mission. My dad explained that he could've
run another one exactly like it the day before and had an entirely
different experience. Because war is fluid, new risks are presented
with every flight. Weather conditions change, enemy troops are
repositioned all the time, and the artillery they are armed with
varies with the particular unit you encounter. This is why the

military demands that *every* mission be devised to include planning, preparation, execution, and assessment stages. In any given situation, it wants its troops to have a process for working through all the options and getting the job done.

The planning stage conditions you to think of all the possible things that could go wrong so you can refine your operational choices to avoid those possibilities. Of course, no one can think of every possibility, but meticulous planning can remove multiple obstacles from your path so you can focus better on the one you hadn't anticipated if and when it arises.

Preparation not only includes gathering every resource you need, it also includes proper training and practice, which is ongoing in the military. This is essential because the rote ability that comes with constant training and preparation enables you to react quickly if and when a plan changes midstream.

The eternal hope for the execution phase is that it goes perfectly according to plan—and if it doesn't, that your constant exposure to planning and preparing has made you flexible enough to devise and execute a successful contingency on the spot.

The assessment stage ensures that whatever challenges you encountered, and the solution you instantly devised to overcome it, get added to the long list of considerations for the next time you set out to plan a mission.

My father's story made an indelible impression on me for several reasons. First, because he survived the attack. Second, because he thought quickly enough to attempt more than one escape route. And third, because it taught me that *it's rare for anyone to just wing it and be successful, even when it looks like they are.* As my dad said then, "You might wonder why you have to go through all this elaborate devising if the moment a plan is initiated it's subject to change. But this elaborate devising is necessary to get you familiar with all the assets and options available to you. That's what the training is all about too. It's how you get good enough to make those on-the-spot decisions that ultimately accomplish the mission."

I walked away from that story with the understanding that success is far less likely without devising a complete mission plan—one that includes a well-thought-out game plan, lots of training, the agility to come up with a contingency on a moment's notice, and the sense to take away a lesson from the experience for future reference.

THINKING A STEP AHEAD

Americans are fascinated by the idea of instant success. We think of certain actors, musicians, athletes, and business moguls as overnight sensations when, in fact, they've often worked for years honing their craft in less visible places before finally arriving in the spotlight. We, as a culture, also vest a lot of faith in positive thinking to help us achieve our goals. Although this will carry you a distance during the toughest leg of your journey, positive thinking alone will not lead you to victory. Every soldier I've ever met knows that you've got to do more than just run out onto the battlefield screaming, "We're going to win!" That right there is a *declaration*, not a plan for success. You've got to plan, prepare, execute, and assess missions countless times before you can let loose that battle cry and really mean it.

"Devise Your Mission" is one of my most essential rules to remember for this reason. It provides a blueprint for winning that's based on substantive planning and training. It focuses you on the necessary and very specific steps you must take to achieve excellence and fulfill your mission. Because it's also realistic, it conditions you to anticipate the challenges along the way, and your possible reactions. If you have already begun to implement all of the rules preceding this one, you are definitely ready to devise your own personal mission plan and make whatever you have been dreaming about a reality.

GIRL WITH A GOAL

Every summer while I was growing up, my cousins and I would go to Texarkana, Texas, to visit my grandmother, whom we called Ma Dear. We would stay with her for weeks at a time enjoying her company and her amazing cooking. It was a leisurely respite from my busy and structured life on base.

I think it was the summer I was about to enter sixth grade when my future aspirations really started to become apparent to others as well as to myself. My cousins were still playing with Barbies, but pretend fashion shows didn't hold my interest for very long anymore. My voice was already deep and my enunciation was crisp from all the reading aloud I did for fun. I would broadcast the dinner menu, narrate the descriptions and reviews I found in the movie section of the newspaper, and I'd tell endless stories to the younger kids and their stuffed animals when it was time for them to fall asleep. I knew I wanted to be a great communicator when I grew up and my voice was already bolder than the voices of other children my age. Being different felt lonely at times, but I tried not to focus on that. Instead I filled up my brain with details about the people I met and the places I had been.

That summer, as I picked peppers alongside Ma Dear in her tiny backyard garden, I told her all about my incessant urge to travel. I said, "All I want to do is journey and collect stories."

I loved her reply, "Well then, you can't stay where you are and be at peace because it seems to me the Lord has put a calling on your heart. He's stirring things up in your soul and soon you will see opportunities come your way. You will travel because He's stirring your nest, too." Then she looked at me and said, "You're lucky you're blessed to know what you are meant to do."

We talked more throughout that visit and it occurred to me that even though she was a civilian she really understood the concept of a mission plan. She knew that when you find your purpose, you absolutely need to live it. And in order to do that, you have to have a plan that includes recognizing opportunities and seizing them. She told me that mostly everyone in her large family was poor, but they understood this concept too. She described them to me as, "some of the most motivated folk you ever wanted to meet." She said, "When one of them caught an idea, it was like fire." She was like that in the kitchen too. She was such a fabulous chef even though she never had a day of formal training. She taught herself to cook until she had learned how to make everything taste flavorful in new and surprising ways. I loved every meal she prepared. But her real, personal mission was raising a half dozen children to become productive, loving, and creative adults, one of whom was my mom. Ma Dear hated one word more than all the rest: *Lazy.* I'm certain that I inherited my work ethic from her.

While I first learned the underlying principles of my "Devise

Your Mission" rule from my father's stories and from observing him and other officers on base, it was in talking with Ma Dear that I truly got a sense of how one applies it to their everyday civilian life and to their long-range goals as well. Her encouragement to pursue my dreams and to never let any obstacle stand in my way contributed greatly to my current success. She had an abundance of perseverance, passing away just days before her one hundred first birthday a few years ago. I'm indebted to her for her common-sense wisdom.

PLAN B

Ma Dear was right. I was lucky that I knew what I wanted to be when I grew up.

The most important mission we will ever embark on is the fulfillment of our life's purpose.

When you are in the military you are told what the objective of your mission is before you are tasked with devising a plan to achieve it. But the rest of us either struggle to discover our most important objective or we have to learn to trust our intuition about it. Some people take years to figure this out, which is unfortunate when you consider that we are only on this planet for a short while and it requires a lot of planning, preparing, executing, assessing, and refining to achieve that one big goal.

Over time, what began for me as a desire to travel the world and tell the stories of the people I met became a burning need to disseminate vital information in a way that helps people look at some pretty difficult situations and still find hope on the other side. Maybe it was growing up in an environment where the prospects for defeat and death were so real that my mission developed into what it is today. But whatever the origins of this twenty-plus-year quest, all I know now is that when darkness is upon us—when serious events occur that leave us all bewildered or searching for understanding—I find it meaningful to be there with the latest details as a point of light for my viewers.

I know that I serve this purpose successfully because people tell me I do. After I delivered the news about the 2012 school shooting at Sandy Hook, for instance, many viewers wrote to tell me that they felt more comforted getting that soul-wrenching news from me because they saw the pain they were feeling in my eyes, too. I was experiencing the same emotions they were. And I needed to hear answers to the same questions they did.

My earliest practice couldn't have hinted at how serious a role journalists play in the lives of others, but it was valuable training nevertheless. I documented *everything* that occurred from my tween years on. I kept loads of composition books filled with notes on every event or subject that caught my attention. I mean those books were filled in the margins and right up through the very last page with notes!

I remember keeping a diary too and announcing to my mother that I was going to lock it up each night so she wouldn't be tempted to read it. Much to my surprise, she just laughed and said, "Honey I love you, but I'm not going to read that. You write *constantly*. I don't have that kind of time." Then she added, "Besides, you talk so much that I already know what's in that diary." I guess you could say that I delivered the daily news of my life to her so she didn't have to seek it out herself.

I also recall how whenever people told me details about what was going on in their lives, I would say, "Oh, that's a great story.

Do you mind if I put that in my diary?" When they said, "No, I don't mind. Go ahead," I'd instantly include what they shared and file it in my journal under lock and key just in case my mother changed her mind about prying. (I knew how important it was that my sources trust me.)

Throughout this book I recount how I went about devising my mission to become the kind of journalist I had always aspired to be. I talk about how I planned and prepared—where I studied, what I majored in, and who some of my biggest influences were. I also talked about how I adopted practices to keep my mind, body, and spirit strong enough to support my goals. I speak of the character traits I continually strive to develop and about the team I lean on most to succeed. In other words, I am teaching you to constantly be nimble so that your preparedness meets the obstacles to victory.

I can see how when one lays it out like this, it looks as if everything went along without a hitch from the earliest of days, but that was not the case at all. It rarely is. Every step I took required a mini mission plan of its own, and you can bet that embedded within each of those mini mission plans was a contingency plan because challenges, roadblocks, and failures are a very real part of the process for everyone—no exceptions.

When I was in Minneapolis at KSTP-TV, for instance, I knew programming experience was necessary to take me to the next level of my career, so I relentlessly pursued my general manager to let me develop my own show. He wanted to support me. He liked my work and didn't want to see me leave any time soon, but his hands were tied. Local news stations don't typically create new programming. There just isn't a place for them to put it. Giving up on this plan, however, was not an option for me. My mother and father didn't raise me that way. And giving up didn't exist in the military mind-set either. *Can you imagine if my dad ever quit on a mission midflight?* That's how lives are lost in battle and that's certainly how dreams die for the rest of us.

My father would always say that if something goes wrong in the sky you have to be able to look through the smoke and say convincingly to yourself, I'm going to make it out of here and I'm still going to hit that target because that is what I trained long and hard to do.

Luckily my GM was as persistent as I was. He came back to me with an idea. The only other platform he had to offer me was radio. Internet programming was in its infancy then. Of course, this wasn't what I originally planned, but I still jumped at the chance because it served my purpose. The idea is to get to the end goal through whatever alternative and appropriate means necessary. So I created a radio program on 107.1 FM with what was a fresh idea at the time—an all-women talk show format. It was called *The Harris Faulkner Show.* I engaged my listeners with motivational content. It aired between the 5:00 P.M. evening and 10:00 P.M. nightly news, both of which I coanchored on TV. It was a little hectic to do both television and radio side by side like that, but the experience was invaluable.

There were other occasions in my career when a job was no longer helping me to grow and I knew a change was definitely in order. Because there are a limited number of anchor positions in any given region, uprooting my life and moving to another city always had to be factored into my contingency plans. If the goal was important enough to me, I knew I had to make the tough decisions and follow through on them, even if it meant leaving trusted colleagues, friends, and a beloved city and viewership behind. Since another of my goals was to keep important people in my life, I knew that I would still find a way to do that too. There were also times when an idea or a proposed innovation never got past "go" for a variety of reasons, from funding and timing to manpower or other resources. I just used lessons from these instances to plan and prepare better for the next time. The experience often fueled a future endeavor that ended up being more exciting and that effectively offset the earlier disappointment.

Even now, I love juggling different projects. I am always looking for ways to expand my knowledge and eagerly seeking fresh ways to create new content and to serve a different role in its dissemination. I enjoy brainstorming with others in the Fox family who are exploring similar opportunities. When these ideas take greater shape, then devising a mission plan is what will catapult all of us to the next level.

The message here is that you should never give up. Success takes practice. In the military, tests are administered before you can rise to the next level. If you fail at first, it's expected that you will try again until you succeed. The same is true in the legal profession, where people take the bar exam as many times as they must until they pass. If you are a student, know that even if it will have no bearing on your grade, you should approach your teacher or professor and ask to take a test again if you believe you could do better a second time around. The effort improves your skills and the initiative improves your character.

The military teaches you that every plan and every contingency must be developed with pinpoint specificity, and this is true. But in broader terms, let me say this: The plan is *always to meet your goal* and the contingency is to *never give up*!

"Devising Your Mission" is absolutely vital to achieving your life purpose. I can't state that strongly enough. It is one of my primary rules, and can be the first one you put into effect in your life or it can be one you explore further down the line, after you have worked on some of the other areas we've discussed so far. But make no mistake about it: This rule is crucial to learn and practice frequently and completely.

I employ it to meet a whole host of other objectives in my daily life. I rely on it so much that I can tick off the boxes of each stage in my mind as I've done them. It's especially ideal for parents. Anyone with children whose extracurricular activities pull them in multiple directions absolutely cannot survive a weekend without a mission plan. That assures all family members are everywhere they're supposed to be on time. Buying or building a home requires a mission plan. Holiday shopping requires a mission plan. Taking your family on vacation requires a mission plan. Every contractor will tell you things go wrong. Every store runs out of its most popular toys in December, and every traveler gets delayed or misses a flight some time or another. Contingencies include hiring people with mission planning skills that far exceed the standard, shopping online a few weeks or months early, and investing in a VIP pass so there's no waiting in line at the theme park once you've finally arrived at your family vacation destination. In other words, there are always options when you plan and prepare and when you remember what hiccups to avoid the next time around.

My dad has been so conditioned to do this by the military that even years after his retirement he still devises a mission plan to head down to the local pharmacy. *How many times have you left the drugstore without getting everything you need?* Military spouses are also great examples of people who use this rule effectively. There are few other people on the planet who can pack up a house, ship everything off to a new location, get their kids settled in yet another school, or juggle being both mom and dad for months at a time better than they can. And they will tell you it's because they do it with a mission plan.

If it sounds like a lot of work, trust me—it takes far less effort than the alternative of digging yourself out from under the mound of problems that pile up when you don't plan, prepare, execute, and assess. The risk-to-reward ratio makes the investment totally worthwhile. I also understand that few of these issues are a matter of life or death. However, devising a plan in civilian life does help to ensure a better *quality* of life. Believe me, you will be in a far better mind-set to succeed at achieving your larger life goals when you're not stressed out.

PURPOSE + HUSTLE = SUCCESS

This whole book, as you know, is intended to help you achieve excellence and success in all the areas you wish to. But for a moment I want to engage you in an exercise designed to help you discover the mother of all goals: *Living your purpose.* Then, together, we'll walk through an example of how you can devise your mission around that purpose.

It may sound daunting at first, but if you've begun to put some of the guidance offered in prior chapters to work, you will be well fortified for this effort.

To all the readers who have identified their life purpose already, please continue to follow along as well. You may find further insight to help you reach that goal, or you may discover a new direction that will lead more efficiently to it. Or perhaps you will find a way to combine one talent with another to supercharge your mission. I suggest this because my father always taught me that the most successful tactic—whether you have ten years, ten days, or ten minutes to devise, prepare, and execute a mission—is to squeeze in as many reviews of your plan as you can before, during, and after the event.

By the way, one of the things I love about the military is that they are actually great at helping their soldiers find a place and purpose. After a new recruit interviews and gets a thumbs-up for having the necessary physical, mental, and ethical attributes, they take a three-hour comprehensive test called the Armed Services Vocational Aptitude Battery (ASVAB). The multiple-choice questions and written components across several disciplines are designed to help match each prospective service member's skills to a branch that could benefit from those skills. This test is followed by a physical exam that helps determine if a recruit has a trait that would negatively impact his or her ability to do a particular job. For example, many jobs require normal color vision to be able to receive signals involving lights or flares. A recruit who is found to have red/green color blindness would naturally be unable to perform those jobs to expectation. Collectively these tests are used to identify the military occupation that best suits each soldier. During basic training, additional opportunities exist to observe how effectively each service member's skills are applied, and to plot his or her further development and career path. The military's success rate is pretty awesome. There are times when troops have resisted their placement, thinking that there were better options for them, only to discover later that they would have been undertasked in those other roles.

In the absence of these kinds of measures in civilian life, you'll have to find your purpose another way. That's where the following questions and prompts come in. Please consider each with care and remember that this is not the time to be modest. Only you will see your answers, so be as honest with yourself as possible.

Begin by constructing a list of your very best skills. It's not quite as objective as taking the ASVAB, but it is a strong start. Really think about what capabilities belong on that list. Leave the list somewhere you can see it for at least a week and add to it as more and more of your talents pop into your head. So many of us take our best skills for granted because they are second nature to us. Giving yourself some time to notice them again in your daily life will ensure that you don't overlook them as possible long-term pursuits.

Continue the process by asking yourself which activities on that list you enjoy doing most of all? What makes you feel happy and productive? Do any of these skills make you feel useful to others?

Then consider all of the activities you engage in that tend to earn you the greatest respect and compliments from the people around you. Their added perspective can help you focus on your best assets. For instance, I am a pretty decent chef. (I get that quality from Ma Dear too!) I'm always baking something and, in fact, before sitting down to write this chapter, I just devoured some guilt-free brownies that I made from vanilla yogurt. Not only do I crave them, but my family and friends ask for them as well, especially when these gooey, addictive treats are topped with an irresistible layer of my homemade Chantilly sauce. So at my loved ones' encouragement, I might put baking or sauce-making on my list, but I would also put several other pursuits I enjoy and excel at on that list.

Be sure to make your list as long and robust as possible, and then look it over carefully. In short order that list will start organizing itself into clearer and clearer priorities.

In my case, it would become apparent that while I am someone whose mini goals include making delectable desserts for those around me, I'm not really a baker or a sauce-maker by trade. Something else on my list would be calling out to me more emphatically as a career.

Over time, all the attributes associated with a storyteller who thrives on sharing relevant and important information with others would naturally top my list of skills. Today it's clear to me, and to most others, that my purpose in life is to do exactly what I am doing. My inner circle knows it and is happy to support my purpose in whatever ways they can. My viewers support it too. My social media feeds are filled with comments from people telling me that they like to hear the news from me because they trust me. I consider their trust an incredible honor. I also consider it a serious responsibility. As a result, I try to live my purpose to its fullest capacity every day. It defines my existence and further shapes my mission.

Is there something others always seem to trust you to do? Are you skilled enough at fixing cars that your friends will ask you to tune up theirs? Do you have such flair and style—not to mention skill with a sewing machine—that your sister has asked you to design and make her wedding dress, veil, or accessories?

As you can see, taking a deep look inside while also paying close attention to the feedback of others can help you identify your purpose too.

By the way, you may find more useful hints in your childhood. Think back to hobbies and potentially untapped talents that have remained with you all along, but have since been glossed over because of all the other obligations you have. Ask your loved ones what they remember about the activities you instinctively gravitated toward in your youth. What impressed them the most? What did they think you were going to be when you grew up? What encouragement did your teachers give you? There may be some wonderful clues about your purpose in their reflections as well as in your own.

Once you've identified your life purpose—as this exercise aims to help you do—think about how often you are actively engaged in living some aspect of it already. I've always believed that when you've found your purpose—and certainly after you've sought proper training for it—you could look at a situation, a room full of people, or a task at hand, and just know that no one else in that room would do it quite the way you would because you'd bring something special to it.

Knowing your purpose is about recognizing your place in the world—the lane you want to drive in better than anybody else. Of course, two or more of us may cruise that lane, but we each do it in a way that makes it uniquely our own. For instance, my husband, who runs his own successful media-relations company, was a great live-shot artist in the news business when we met. He definitely knew his way around that lane. In fact, that's my joke—when I met my Tony I got my first Emmy, because learning from him made me a better live-shot artist too. Although we both enjoyed success in the same business, I had developed a different on-air skill. When it comes to breaking news, I'm quite good at sitting calmly in a chair while millions of people watch, processing reports and videos regarding an unfolding situation as they trickle in, and talking to the corners of those images for the benefit of our viewers until I've helped make some sense of it all. Somehow, I can always find a way to draw the audience in with what we do know, and not pontificate or extrapolate anything, but just be in the moment intuiting the right thing to say. My husband is a great storyteller—better than I am—but he doesn't have *that* particular skill. That unique ability to ad-lib, to go into extemporaneous talk mode for an extended period of time until more and more details are organically unveiled. That's a very specific skill and that's the lane I like driving in.

You can see this principle at work in other fields. For instance, there are certainly other clergymen out there in the world, but few understand their purpose and live it quite like Bishop T. D. Jakes. Jakes founded the nondenominational megachurch, The Potter's House, in Dallas, Texas. He speaks to women's issues so compellingly that he has his own show on the Oprah Winfrey Network.

Is there anyone who really inspires you? If so, why? Is theirs a lane you might consider driving in as well?

Take Action

Once you have determined the lane you belong in, you'll want to plan how you will navigate it all the way to the point of success, including reaching each scheduled milestone along the way. You'll prepare for getting there with proper training. You'll execute your plan, and of course, should you get stalled along the way, you'll assess the obstacles in your path and, like the Waze app, you'll find the best means to get around them. That's not just the way the military devises a mission; it's how *you* should devise all your missions going forward.

Love at first sight! My mom, Shirley Harris, and me, October 1965.

Eight-month-old me with Mom in suburban Atlanta, Georgia.

My dad, Bob Harris, during his elementary school days;
Dad's high school graduation picture, 1955;
My parents on their wedding day, December 20, 1959.

My newlywed parents.

My mom's passport. She told me she could
not have imagined taking the official photo
without me.

Three-year-old me with Mom in Ludwigsburg, Germany. I loved the view from the flight
control elevator of Dad's airplane.

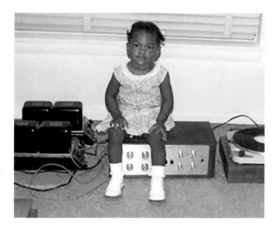

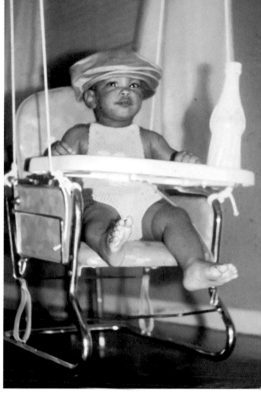

Taking a rest on moving day, leaving Fort McPherson assignment for Stuttgart. Military families relocate a lot!

One-year-old me, donning one of my dad's favorite caps, in Atlanta, Georgia.

Military quarters playground in Ludwigsburg, Germany, just north of Stuttgart.

Prekindergarten me outside our military quarters in Ludwigsburg, Germany.

Dad in front of Ninth Division headquarters at Long Thanh North Airfield, Vietnam.

Dad as a commander at the avionics repair station in Nha Trang, Vietnam.

My father presenting a young Vietnamese woman with a certificate of appreciation for the work she did to help the US Army during the Vietnam War in Nha Trang.

Dad flying over Vietnam to inspect a landing zone.

Dad outside the barracks at 210th Combat Aviation Battalion,
Long Tranh North, Vietnam.

US soldiers interacting with locals.

Dad in command.

Dad during his second tour of duty in Vietnam.

Street views of Saigon.

Dad during the war in Vietnam.

My parents at an officers' gathering.

Climbing trees in our nation's capital when Dad was working at the Pentagon.

Me as a high school junior in Northern California.

My dad with his civilian special forces back in the day (the 1970s): my uncles Ronnie Lane and Tim Lane.

Dad walking me down the aisle on my wedding day, April 12, 2003.

Mom and my close friend Ed Crony teamed up to help make my wedding day sparkle. Together they accomplished every "squad goal" on their list!

Me and my husband, Tony (aka my number-one special force).

Grandpa Bob with newborn
Bella, December 2006.

Danika's baptism day,
August 2009.
(Photo courtesy of Michelle Burley)

Love you, sister. Danika (six days
old) and Bella (two).

Fascination with the *Intrepid* runs in the family! (*Intrepid* was deployed on two tours in Vietnam.)

Danika and Bella busy "devising their mission" for the perfect day of play.

My mom, Shirley, with her mom, Queen Temple, (aka MaDear).

The girls moments before their television debut on *Fox & Friends*. Meteorologist Rick Reichmuth helps keep them happy and calm.

Us "owning our moment" after a long hike to the Hudson River's iconic Little Red Lighthouse. (*Photo by Tatiana Kiseleva*)

Selfies with talk-show host Montel Williams who "watched my six" after a stalker threatened me, and with retired four-star Army general Jack Keane who mentors us on how to "think like a general" in Rule #7 of this book!

Subway poster of my first Fox News show in primetime, *Fox Report Weekend*.

About to launch my own daily Monday–Friday show, *Outnumbered Overtime with Harris Faulkner*, October 2, 2017.

Some of my loving family members at the Afterglow reception my parents held in memory of my Aunt Mary in September 2016. My mom passed away shortly thereafter.

Arriving at Glamour Women of the Year Awards in 2017.

On set of my Fox News show, *Outnumbered Overtime with Harris Faulkner*, 2018.

Let's look at how this would play out if, for example, you wanted to be even more of a baker than I'm prepared to be (aka a supremely *professional* one rather than an *amateur* one.) I use this analogy because dabbling in it as a hobby has taught me a little bit more about it than most other endeavors, except obviously broadcast journalism.

When devising your mission, remember to be as specific as you can. In order to craft the ideal plan, you must state your goal up top. Is it your desire to someday be the *best* baker in the world? Can you name who that person is today? How does one even define the *best* in this field of endeavor? Is it your aim to actually place at the Coupe du Monde de la Boulangerie (literally the world cup for bakers)? Do you want to run a place more like the Dominique Ansel Bakery in New York City, the Tatte in Boston, or the pâtisserie Sadaharu AOKI in Tokyo and Paris? (These are currently considered among the top bakeries in the universe!) Or do you much prefer to bring your confections to dessert lovers via a restaurant, catering service, or trendy food truck?

After you define success for yourself, you can proceed to investigate the different paths the bakers you most admire have taken to achieve their current status. From their experiences and wisdom, you will get a reasonable idea of how long it will take you to achieve a similar goal. You will set an end date by which you aim to meet your goal. You will look into the various culinary schools, online courses, and websites that can teach you all of the necessary techniques and recipes. Again, you will note the series of milestones you'll need to meet before arriving at your final goal date.

Prepare

You will proceed by training in every way possible—in controlled situations and in the field. In other words, you will actually enroll in a culinary school, or seek an apprenticeship with a master baker/pastry maker/culinary artist near you or at a bakery of your choice. You will make profiteroles, tarts, cupcakes, and just about everything else that elicits raves from friends, family, and strangers. You will offer to bake for a local fundraising event so you can benefit from the added experience. You will contact a favorite magazine or blog and volunteer to test recipes for them. You will enter contests—maybe even one on the Food Network. And if you are truly daring, you will send your local newspaper's food or restaurant critic some delectables made just for him. His feedback will be invaluable.

Execute

After planning and preparing to achieve your goal, you will finally enact it. You'll work hard, sometimes rising the way military people do at zero dark thirty (aka 5:30 A.M.) to be sure your freshly mixed popover batter is in the oven on time for the breakfast rush. You'll keep your specific career goal in mind at all times. Did you decide to establish a bakery, a restaurant beloved for its desserts, a catering service, or a trendy food cart or truck of your own? Or did you decide to work your magic at an already established and popular eatery where you are sure to garner attention? Will you put your skills to slightly different use and perhaps develop the tastiest low-calorie desserts Weight Watchers or Jenny Craig has ever offered to their clientele? You've done the research; you know the lane you're in, and you've planned how to cruise that lane in your own style, so don't be afraid to be different. Strike out and do whatever it is you have carefully planned and prepared to do.

Assess

Has anything you've tried not worked? Although yours is a time-tested art, don't forget to think about how new developments can help you revise your approach. Remember: Review, review, review. Are you fluent in all the ways the digital world can help you expand your craft and business? Are you using new kitchen technologies to your best advantage? Have you fully explored and informed yourself about all the options? Are you reaching high enough? If not, simply make time for changes. You will remain poised throughout this entire process to assess your progress and make whatever adjustments to your plan that are required to assure you rise to success the way your best dough recipe does. You will naturally add a pinch more of this or a pinch more of that to perfect your confections.

If there are times when you struggle with one too many fallen soufflés (in other words, when you experience mission failure), think again about the example of my dad and other military men and women. Failure is not an option for them. They can't afford to just give up and quit. And frankly, after your investment of time, energy, and money, you can't either. You simply need to rethink and reset your plan. There is no shame in that.

After seeing how devising your mission works in a career situation such as the one above, you are now ready to apply the same principle steps to every other objective you wish to achieve in your life. I don't know about you, but I see hashtag goals all over Twitter these days. There are #workgoals, #marriagegoals, and #fitnessgoals to name a few. And, of course, #yolo, reminding each of us that we only live once. Think about how it will feel to add #victory and #doneanddone to your social media feeds, then do it.

Even after you have arrived at your goals and enjoyed the sweet and savory results of your labor, be sure to revisit and revise your mission(s) every now and then so you are always expanding your possibilities and gaining new skills.

I know I used an example from the kitchen instead of from the battlefield, but the lessons really are the same. If you hunger to succeed you need a detailed plan that will give your efforts a fighting chance.

Here again, very succinctly, is the military's recipe for successfully devising your mission along with my own recipe for helping you define your most important objective.

FOR YOUR OBJECTIVE

Fold the following ingredients together:

- Any special skills you possess
- Past and present interests and hobbies
- Activities that are most gratifying to you
- Things you do that are useful to others
- Things people unconditionally *trust* you to do
- Your childhood intuition
- Early encouragements from family and friends
- Inspiration you get from the work others do

Let sit and gel.

FOR THE MISSION

- Plan
- Prepare
- Execute
- Assess

Set a timer with firm deadlines for each stage.
Complete the mission and enjoy.

Rule #5

WEAR CAMO

Dress blues certainly turn heads. They elicit a lot of respect from people. They're great-looking uniforms, especially when they are worn by highly decorated officers. All those ribbons and medals are impressive. But for my money, the go-to option if you really want to *dress for success* in the military is camo. It's the hardest working outfit in the armed services.

During the Vietnam War the pattern was windblown leaves. It was worn to blend into the native foliage. Infantrymen would often apply black, brown, and green cream on their faces and on the exposed skin of their necks and hands. They'd also tuck grass, leaves, twigs, and whatever other natural materials they could find in their helmets as further concealment. They would take special care to cover anything that could reflect sunlight too—even just small glints of it.

As a pilot, my father kept his attire to basic camo. None of these extras were necessary for him. Most times he had to worry more about hiding his plane when he had touched ground. A few of the aircrafts he flew had countershading, but on the day he had a close call with the enemy on an open airfield, his plane wasn't hidden, nor was it painted in anything other than dark green to make it less visible. He had landed on a small strip, dropped off special munitions, and delivered an intelligence person to a unit waiting beyond the airfield as his orders directed him to do. He was returning to the plane when he spotted a squad of seven to nine Vietcong soldiers on the terrain just below him. To this day he cannot imagine why they didn't approach the plane to check it out. They had to have seen it. It's pretty hard to miss something that size when it's sitting just a couple hundred yards away. He was also baffled as to why they didn't search for him. Someone had to have piloted that thing. It still mystifies him as to why they just kept going. Did they really have someplace more important to be? He was sure that he saw them scanning the edges of the field before they walked away. They had to have noticed him then. But as sure as he is about that, I'm sure that they didn't. It's by the grace of God that they chose to move past that plane that day, but I think it was also by the grace of camo that they never spotted him.

He quickly completed what he set out to do, hopped back on that plane, and hightailed it out of there.

We often think of "dressing for success" as wearing something that gets us noticed rather than something that helps us get the job done. There is definitely a time and a place for being recognized and the military has a whole protocol for that. (I set aside an entire chapter on that topic.) "Appearing in your best light and dressing to reflect the discipline and success of the military" is definitely something that is stressed at every level of command. No institution I know of teaches meticulous attention to detail in one's attire and every other aspect of behavior than the armed services do. But there are other ways to design and use what you wear to achieve mission success before you celebrate and reflect that success in your clothing.

POWER DRESSING

More than concealing one's position, camo enables troops to adapt to their environment. It often buys them time to scope out the advantages and disadvantages of their surroundings and to consider the use and avoidance of those advantages and disadvantages accordingly. This is just one of the many subtle and complex ways the military understands and treats attire as a tool. It has designed many different types of uniforms that serve different purposes in different situations for exactly this reason. It has also subjected these uniforms to rigorous testing. The military knows there is more to dressing for success and certainly more to wearing camo than meets the eye.

This rule is on my list of top nine because it reminds me to consider the different ways I can use attire to my advantage, increasing my chances to excel at what I do. There are times when you must use your wardrobe to do more than just appear to be successful; you must use it to actually achieve that success.

HATS OFF TO CAMO!

Wearing camouflage gave me power from a very early age. My mother would dress me in my dad's officer's cap when he was deployed and she was missing him. Seeing me in that hat gave her power as well. It lifted her spirits and helped her focus on the things she needed to do in his absence. The cap had what was called "scrambled eggs" on the front of it. The scrambled eggs referred to the gold braiding that boldly stands out. By the time my father was first deployed to Vietnam he was already a captain and his attire had changed, so he left this cap behind. Watching me wear that hat revived Mom's heart and brought a bright smile to her face.

Military families may not be in a bunker alongside the soldier they love, but they are serving too. Our job is to keep positive and hopeful thoughts and pour them into letters and rare phone calls to those in the field (aka the battlefield). Sometimes when my mom needed to feel strong, she would sit with the few military items Dad left behind. She told me years later that as a toddler I loved donning that oversized camouflaged cap—that wonderful cap with the lingering scent of our household hero.

My mother felt the power of positive thinking looking at me in that hat. And wearing it as a baby apparently made me feel closer to the man I barely knew yet. Mom used to remind me that how we dress tells the world what is important to us. Wearing that hat told the world my dad was a valuable member of our family and that we missed him. Other simple yet salient examples of how people do this in special circumstances can be seen in a remnant from home tied to a refugee's shirt; a pink ribbon or accessory worn by someone in solidarity with a mother, sister, daughter, or friend who is fighting breast cancer; or a black armband worn by a person of Jewish faith who is mourning a loved one.

To this day I own an inordinate amount of camouflaged clothing. It is a fashion statement for many people, but for me it is a welcome reminder to cultivate and protect my positivity and hope.

BEST SUITED FOR THE JOB

On Memorial Day of 2017 I was reminded of the importance of camo once again. As I mentioned in an earlier chapter, I was aboard the USS *Kearsarge* (LHD 3) commemorating the lives of the servicemen and -women who fought for us over the years and died in the line of duty. My young daughters, Bella and Danika, were with me and so were hundreds of military personnel from the different branches of the armed forces. These various soldiers and sailors were there to help man the ship in the waters of the Hudson River for the numerous guests who were visiting. Many of these servicemen and -women were in town for Fleet Week and had volunteered to be on duty knowing what an honor working aboard the *Kearsarge* would be. This particular vessel is the fifth amphibious assault ship to bear the same name as the iconic battleship of the Civil War. Over time, the name has become synonymous with the best of what the United States has in its armada. This particular *Kearsarge* boasts a highly sophisticated antiaircraft defense system among many other impressive features.

Considering how many branches of the military were represented that day, it was hard not to notice all the assorted uniforms, especially the array of camouflage. On deck were military personnel wearing several variations on a theme. Colors and patterns differed depending upon where that soldier was typically stationed.

When the service members stood in line, the girls and I looked up and down the row and counted six different versions. Among them were shades of blue from slate and pale blue to dark navy. There were also beige and brown combinations and more familiar mixes of woodland greens.

When we spoke to a few of the soldiers they explained the reason for the differences. If the fight is in the deep blue ocean off the coast of Yemen, then deep blue will be the overtone of your camouflage. You can't risk being spied by an enemy sniper while you're standing on deck, even if that sniper is at a distance. You've got to blend into the background, whatever that background may be. If you were in Desert Storm, Kuwait, or Afghanistan, your uniform was the color of earth or sand. In other locations where we are fighting ISIS, the terrain may call for wearing a mix of darker greens and browns. As one marine said, "You dress according to what the battle lines look like."

I took that comment in for a second and began to see the even greater power of camo. It became clear that it's not only about hiding in plain sight or about adapting. It is also about *consciously bringing a different approach or strategy to the environment you are in.*

If your first instinct is to interpret the phrase "dress for success" as looking your best or standing out in a crowd, you would quickly rethink that interpretation based upon what these troops said. Likewise, you wouldn't only think of camo as a tool to help you blend in. These definitions are correct, but they aren't the only ones that apply.

I started going through my wardrobe in my head and separating what I call *impression-wear* from *mission-wear.*

Impression-wear, to me, is what we wear when we really want

to stand out or command attention, respect, or recognition. It is also what we wear when we want to send a message. How we dress is a personal language that we speak. It communicates so much about us, from our emotions to our aspirations. It not only reflects our current success, it hints at where we see ourselves in the future.

Mission-wear, on the other hand, is what we wear to enable us to do our job or complete a mission well. It doesn't always have to be understated, but it is something that adapts to our situation. It is also something that is chosen with a lot of forethought about how it is needed or will be useful in our specific environment.

There are some obvious examples of mission-wear in professions that require uniforms for very particular reasons. Athletes' uniforms, for instance, are designed for comfort, protection, and performance. Their uniforms also brand them as part of the same team. Surgeons wear freshly laundered scrubs for sanitary reasons. Nurses in pediatric units often wear more brightly colored or playfully patterned uniforms to help lift their patients' spirits. Clothes that are designed specifically for our work let others know we're serious about the roles we are fulfilling. It's clear to see in these instances how our attire enables us to do our jobs well.

Of course, there will be times when impression-wear and mission-wear can be mixed and matched to help you do your job better. For instance, a lot of us in the media dress to impress for work. Television is, after all, a visual medium. How we look plays a big role in our appeal to the public. But I also give a lot of thought to how my choice of clothes will actually enhance the way I communicate and connect with my audience and interview subjects. The seriousness of the news I deliver dictates style and color. This was especially true for the more than six years when

I was in primetime on *Fox Report Weekend*. Some color theorists believe that certain hues signal trust, fairness, balance, and even hope. Since I strive to possess and project those qualities through my actions and words, it's natural that I aim to send the same message through my clothes as well.

Each week, I also manage the wardrobe color wheel for Fox News Channel's daytime program *Outnumbered*. It's one of the many things I do behind the scenes as cohost. On Sunday evenings, I coordinate the outfit colors for the upcoming week's shows. The point is to avoid duplication and to be sure that my colleagues, who are all beautiful, poised, intelligent women, appear as individual as their editorial viewpoints. As we challenge the "guy in the middle" who joins us to analyze and explore some of the most complex and relevant political, social, and cultural issues of that day, we don't want there to be any distractions. As I joke: Twinning is not winning. We want to all be on an equal playing field, appearing as confident as we truly are, dressed in the power colors of our choice, and exuding complete comfort and respect for each other and ourselves. Wearing the right mix can subtly reinforce the ways we all complement each other as well as the ways we are all unique. Bottom line: We do not want anyone looking at the screen and thinking, *Bridesmaids*!

Despite making a distinction between what I refer to as mission-wear and impression-wear, I do find that dress uniforms—those worn for special occasions in the military—fall into both categories because they definitely inspire respect and call attention to the wearer, but that is also what they are designed to do. It is, in part, their function, or job. The uniform's formality reflects the integrity and values of the military and the insignias, medals, and decorations reflect the excellence of each individual wearer. I cannot tell you how formidable my father looked on occasions when he wore his dress uniform. Nothing projects an air of success, discipline, and achievement quite like a man or woman wearing theirs proudly.

Today when I see a service member in uniform—whether it is a combat, dress or everyday uniform—it stirs emotions of pride and gratitude and I do think that is an important part of its purpose. I imagine that the wearer feels that way and that most civilians who understand the sacrifice and commitment it represents feel that way too.

My father recently saw a woman in uniform and stopped to salute her. She was uncertain at first as to why he did that. He smiled and said, "Oh but for the moment you outrank me." With the quiet understanding that he had also served at one time, she returned the smile. It's not something he typically does, but seeing people in uniform brings up those same emotions I just mentioned, though perhaps more deeply for him, and he felt like expressing them in the moment.

"Today's troops volunteer because they have pride," he said to me. "When you join the military now, you are essentially saying, 'I raise my right hand to do whatever it is that my country asks me to do—*not* because my country asked me to raise my right hand.'" These were the same intentions he had when he volunteered as a young man.

Of course, uniforms in his day conjured up different feelings for some. There were soldiers in that war who did not go entirely of their own volition. The draft was in effect, as mentioned earlier, so they were conscripted and had little choice in the matter. When they wore their uniform here in the United States, some were made to feel shame for being a part of such an unpopular and misunderstood war. Once when my father was coming home from Vietnam dressed in his, he passed through the Chicago airport and deeply felt the strain of people's disapproval. But he told me he still wore his uniform with pride. He was a representative of the United States in it. He had hoped, though, that it was not seen as a display of opposition to the protest groups, as he didn't wear it with that intent. He has said, "Believe me, there are things I disagreed with our country about." He has also said, "Rightly or wrongly, there were tasks I did not question at the time. But later, when I gathered enough information and saw that things could have been done differently, I knew the structure ought to change and that we had to coordinate that change—but not in a disrespectful way. That is what the uniform is all about."

It is easy to see from this example and others that sometimes what we wear elicits different feelings, in different situations, at different times, and in different people.

THE GO-ANYWHERE OPTION

Although the concept of wearing camo in everyday life—the idea that you consider and choose the best clothes to help you get the job done—can be applied in so many different kinds of situations, this is a rule that works particularly well for those times when you find yourself in new surroundings. It is a good practice to remember when you are starting a new job, enrolling in a new school, or when you are moving to a new neighborhood. You want to make a good visual impression in all of these scenarios, but you also want to bring your best strategy for succeeding in these places too.

Metaphorically wearing camo in a crisis situation—meaning coming armed with your best ideas and attitude—is especially important. I'm referring to those times when you or someone you love is facing a medical challenge and you are uncertain how to proceed. On occasions such as this, when we're not as prepared for life-changing moments as we'd hope to be, anticipating our needs or packing the right positive and determined mind-set can help the transition. Those are the times when we need to embrace the underlying principles of using camo most. The times when we have to scope out our new situation by doing some serious reconnaissance to find out how to best combat the threat. It's when we may need to bring a new kind of thinking to the challenge. When we need to rely on more layers of protection than usual—including family, friends, and neighbors. It's when we need to seek out experts and/or specialists to help us acclimate and reach our goals in this new and foreign milieu. I know that when my father was being treated for his esophageal condition and when my mother was undergoing care for cancer, we went deep into reconnaissance, looking into the best options, the best facilities, the best doctors, and the best practices to support their recovery. We were not only wearing camo, but we were calling for backup, too. We contacted everyone we could think of who knew about or survived the same illnesses to find out more about what we could do to help. Figuring out the lay of the land was crucial in those early days. We scrambled to understand where we were at, what the battle ahead might look like, and what we needed to bring to the fight to cope, endure, and prevail. The combined power of wearing camo and calling upon our special forces really helped.

In retrospect there were probably many times in my life when I was wearing camo and didn't even realize it. The more challenges you face and the more experience you develop overcoming them, the more extensive your camo wardrobe is likely to be. That was clearly reflected on the deck of the *Kearsarge* that Memorial Day as our exceptional servicemen and -women in the US military wore so many different variations of it. They were not just dressed for any occasion; they were clearly dressed for success.

YOUR OWN RECON READY-TO-WEAR

While camo is vogue in the fashion world right now, there are more ways to rock it in your life than by just wearing it. You can use its underlying principles to assess and plan for creating positive changes in your life. The first step is to do some surveillance. Serious surveillance.

Have you taken a close look at your circumstances, your priorities, your goals, your challenges, your relationships, your job, your influences, your home, your finances, or your overall environment lately?

Have you asked yourself if you have the resources necessary to navigate the terrain in these important areas? Are you packing too light? Or do you have all the necessary equipment you need?

What more could you use? Is there anything you are employing that is outdated or in need of repair? Are there new tools that can help you succeed in these areas better, faster, or more efficiently?

Or conversely, are you a gearhead who carries way more flashy equipment or accessories than what the job requires? Showy stuff that only impresses other gearheads while it weighs you down?

Really step outside of yourself and do some serious investigating. Who are the people succeeding in these areas and what are they doing that you may not be doing? Who are the people floundering in this area and what are they doing that you definitely want to avoid doing?

If things are working well for you, ask if they could possibly work better. How and with what tools?

Have you met your goals yet? Or even exceeded them? If so, when was the last time you set new ones?

If you've got your camo on, you can poke around and really look at parts of your life that usually resist introspection.

Even if you have been in one place for a while and are quite comfortable, it's still time to scout around. The world is changing all the time. Is there something you never noticed before? Or just as important, has something you took for granted disappeared while you weren't looking? What do these changes mean for you? Will their presence or absence help or hinder you?

For those of you who think you know your environment already like the back of your hand, periodic recon is still worth doing as it will alert you to any unanticipated challenges. It's possible to miss both large and small changes when we are racing past them every day, distracted by our daily obligations.

Now that you see your surroundings with fresh eyes, do you notice any new opportunities or resources that can help you advance your goals?

If you are new to a situation, I especially encourage you to take a closer look around. Observe and contemplate the challenges your new situation poses. Note the unique advantages it presents too. Are there friendlies or special forces you can recruit to help you navigate or accelerate your adjustment to this new terrain? Are your orders clear? Did you set your objectives before or after taking a measure of the site? Again, what's in your go-kit to help you cope?

Remember camo is not just clothes and equipment. It's anything that can be used effectively. Paola Harrell, for instance, told me that as a black woman and the wife of an officer who had to frequently interact with high-level military personnel, she carried with her the facts that she was a third-generation college graduate, the daughter of university professors, and an engineer to use to her advantage when necessary. This was during the early 1960s so that kind of camo was very effective indeed.

What exactly do you see when you enter your walk-in closet?

Do you have what others have used to successfully thrive in your situation or environment?

Separate the mission wear from the impression wear. The fancy stuff from the really useful stuff. The functional items and the durables from everything else.

Can anything do double duty? You know, are there tools, accessories, attributes, or qualities that can get the job done and also make you look good? If so, shift those to the middle of the rack.

Now looking carefully at what you've lined up neatly in front of you, ask yourself if you have the right camo for the job ahead of you, whatever that may be. Are your options flexible and adaptable enough to suit the situation or task you are facing? Are you making only the obvious choices? Or are there other choices that with more forethought would serve you better? What else do you need to add?

Dressing for success does indeed mean dressing for the occasion or dressing to captivate the attention of higher-ups. It does indeed mean looking the part of a leader before others recognize you as one. It's okay to scrutinize the impression-wear side of the clothes rack to see if you have the accoutrements to do that or if you even own a power suit. (By the way, what does a power suit actually look like in your social circle or field of work? Aspiring rock stars and trial attorneys definitely have different ideas about that.)

But, as we've discussed, it also means considering the usefulness and effectiveness of what you have at your disposal. It means accounting for whether you are in midair, on land, or at sea, so to speak. Wearing camo essentially means asking yourself: "Do I have a strong strategy in place to be where I am—in the battle I am presently in? Did I bring the right stuff to support that strategy?"

If your answer is yes to both questions, congratulations—you are officially rocking camo.

Rule #6

UNLEASH THE POWER OF INTEGRITY

My father was fortunate to have several commanders in his career whom he admired for their integrity. One of the first who impressed him with this quality was his commander in Stuttgart, Germany. His name was Colonel Minkler. My father remembers him as someone whom he could talk to openly. He has said, "There was a lot that went on in the units I was leading. It was important that my commander have total confidence in what I was telling him, and he did. He was a man who understood the value of honesty and truthfulness. He was not interested in being told only what he wanted to hear. He depended on me as I depended on him and I did not want to disappoint. You also never had to reintroduce yourself to him after your initial meeting. He remembered the men under his direction and treated them with respect." And that's not all my father appreciated about him. This fine leader assisted my dad in going to Georgia Tech for his master's degree while he was still serving. What is so remarkable about this is that it occurred in 1964. Mutual respect between a white man in authority and a black man essentially working for him wasn't guaranteed where my father came from. That my dad found it in his first commander was incredibly inspiring, and only deepened his devotion to this man and to the military.

My father also told me many times that Colonel Don Jersey, his commander in Vietnam, was a man of much integrity as well. You will recall that after a stranger set off an explosive that damaged our home and terrified my mother and me into moving, my father was desperate to return to Dallas to be sure we were okay and to see that we had settled into our new environment safely. Unfortunately, he was denied that leave of absence, but he remained convinced that if the colonel—who was away on a covert mission at that time—had known about my father's situation and had spoken to the Red Cross on his behalf, he would have been granted permission without hesitation. Not only did Colonel Jersey have that kind of authority, but his word meant that much to those who knew him. If he vouched for you, there was no doubt that you deserved it. When the colonel returned to the base and heard what had happened, it angered him that my father had been treated unfairly, and he made that displeasure known to everyone involved. Don Jersey's response showed my father that all the extra effort he had put in under the colonel's command did not go unnoticed. A man of integrity rewards good work. He can be firm and demanding, but when the situation warrants it, he responds with understanding and compassion. He can put himself in another's shoes and imagine how he would want to be treated in those same circumstances. Because of the way Colonel Jersey consistently conducted himself, he inspired allegiance from his men and definitely from my dad. I've heard my father say, "I loved that man; I would do anything for him, and he felt, I think, the same of me." Because my father is a man of integrity too, I have no doubt that was true.

Of course, I don't want to sugarcoat the topic. Being a person of integrity is not always easy and it's certainly not always met with immediate gratitude either. For instance, one of my father's duties as his unit's commanding officer when he was stationed in Nha Trung was to patrol a border fence that separated the troops from the local Vietnamese people. All too often illicit activities would occur along that fence. Drugs were sold to the soldiers there and, although it required some interesting maneuvering, troops engaged in sexual relations through the fence too. Because my dad lived close to the edges of the base and so did his men, he felt he had to take a tough stance against this behavior. And he didn't care who knew it. Although some of the other commanders who rotated their watch with my father might have been tempted to look the other way from time to time, he was always vigilant about stopping this conduct. Some kind of control had to be exhibited to keep that fence from being used in ways that compromised the safety of the base. He couldn't afford for those troops to be intoxicated or high at the wrong time. If the base got hit, he had to be sure everyone there was ready for duty. That kind of activity degraded the unit's ability to respond quickly.

His reinforcement of order wasn't popular, but it was as much about making sure no one contracted a disease or was sold bad drugs as it was about readiness. He cared about his soldiers' well-being. To deal with the situation, he'd look his men directly in the eye and say, "You know what this calls for? This calls for jail time if you're caught, and I can't afford that. *We* can't afford that." His objective was to keep those men off that fix no matter what it took. Even if it meant reminding them that one day they'd go back home to their mothers. He told me it angered people when he said that, but it kept them out of harm's way.

The behavior was shocking to him at first, but as soon as you uncover something detrimental you have no time for disbelief; you have to get over the surprise and act swiftly to correct the situation. One of the ways he did so was to become like a father figure to these young men. Many of them were just eighteen or nineteen years old, and frankly they looked even younger than that. My dad was barely ten years older than most of them, but understanding what the stresses of war can do to someone, he had to assume the maturity and perspective they didn't have in the moment and steer them as far away from unhealthy escapes as possible. Luckily, he had been cultivating that maturity for a while. By the time he was twenty-three, he had the responsibility of fifty-six men, all of whom were different ages. When he speaks to young commanders in the military today, he is struck by how many of the twenty-four- or twenty-five-year-olds he meets seem as if they are in their thirties. Responsibility, like the kind they carry every day, makes you grow up fast.

My father was reluctant to share this story with me. I know it casts a light on human fragility when what I want to express in this book is all the ways in which we can be strong enough to meet our goals. But I also think it speaks well to the subject of this chapter. My dad used his own integrity to maintain the integrity of the camp and to help restore the integrity of his men as best he could. The realities of war—and even civilian life at times—would break more people if it were not for those with enough integrity to go around. When people exhibit this trait persistently, it can and often does inspire others to be their best selves too—or at least, a much-improved self. I'm sure those my father kept straight back then appreciated his determination in the long run and recognized the results such character and perseverance can achieve.

THE HONEST TRUTH

Ask people what the word *integrity* means to them and most will say it is when you are honest or trustworthy. Some might venture further to say it is when you live by a moral code or when you have high standards. Integrity is all of this to me. But these definitions just barely scratch the surface of its full meaning. It also refers to people with ideals and goals who don't quit just because things get tough. It's a quality that you either possess or you don't. There is no middle ground. It's either laced through every part of your being or it's not there at all. It is so consistently a part of who you are that it is most effectively defined as *what you do even when you think no one is watching . . . It is what you do for others when they can offer you nothing more than their company in return.* Simply put, *it's doing something just because it's the right thing to do.*

"Unleashing the Power of Integrity" is on my list of rules to live by because it will give you the confidence to know you are on the right path even when you feel out of step with others. It is also on my list because the world really needs more displays of this quality. Those who do not yet possess it can learn from your example and work to acquire and embrace it in their own lives.

RISK/REWARD

I loved hearing my father talk about people he admired even if I hadn't met them yet. But it is quite another experience to put a face with the qualities or the deeds he spoke about. That was what happened when I came across a picture of my father and another officer presenting a young Vietnamese woman with a certificate acknowledging the military's appreciation for her work. It was common for uniformed officers to hire civilian locals to type, file, take dictation, and of course to assist in translating interviews or documents. Many were skilled linguists familiar with English as well as their own and other culture's languages. Most had worked in corporate settings before the war and could be relied on to be dedicated and accurate. They lived in villages where American forces were reaching out to civilians in an effort to change hearts and minds through employment. My father said the interview process involved "extreme vetting" as only the most trustworthy people could be accepted. Women took incredible risks in applying for these jobs and certainly while working in them. They left themselves open to being marked by the enemy, the Vietcong. Sometimes things would happen outside of the office and the applicants or workers would not return the next day. Thoughts ran to the worst-case scenarios. My father told me some of the saddest moments in the war for him were when he and his fellow officers would learn that there was a sudden need to replace one of the women who had become critical components to the war in unit leadership. He said, "They had integrity and they were brave. That is a winning combination and all too often a fatal one." They rarely talked about their personal lives. The vetting process revealed those details for them. Instead they were focused on doing their job, which was to help American soldiers.

There is a lot to learn about the power of integrity from people who risked everything to help those they believed were doing the right thing. Dad said, "It is the kind of weapon every one of us should deploy, especially when people least expect it." The young woman in the picture made quite an impression on me. I was a teenager just about ready to enter college when I first saw the photo. She did not look that much older than me. To the Vietnamese women who endangered their own lives to help soldiers like my dad, please know that I still draw upon your history and the example of extreme integrity you set.

NEWS FLASH

While I comprehended what my father said about "using integrity when people least expect it," true understanding of a concept happens when you actually apply it.

Journalists tend to meet people at their lowest points. Reporters are routinely inserted into emotionally charged situations yet are expected to get to the heart of a story instantly. It's absolutely astonishing that we aren't cussed out more frequently for our apparent impatience. In pursuit of a sound bite that says it all, our questions can often be blunt and seemingly insensitive.

Nothing brought this tendency into clearer focus than when my Minneapolis local TV employer dispatched me to South Africa to cover the AIDS crisis. It was shortly after my wedding and a very happy time for me personally. What greeted me in the post-apartheid villages and shanty divisions of the major cities in

South Africa was mind-blowing—and not in a good way. In the township of Gugulethu alone, the community was putting loved ones in the ground by the thousands. There, every Saturday, fifteen hundred people were buried in mass funerals in a square at the center of town. Even more disheartening were the bizarre and cruel beliefs that spread widely throughout the region about the ways one could beat the odds of getting AIDS. The villagers actually thought that having sex with a little girl—a virgin—could spare one of the dreaded disease. As a result, young girls were being raped—and if that wasn't bad enough, this sexual abuse was putting them at high risk of contracting the virus themselves. At the same time, many local leaders questioned the scientific research behind the treatments that were being offered by Western doctors. This resulted in the poorest citizens being denied life-saving antiretroviral drugs. These were black people, my shade or darker, still forced because of segregation to live outside of Cape Town, where they couldn't access the same health care as those who lived in the bigger cities. The stories of heartbreak and death were endless. It was exhausting, but being there to witness and share their story was important.

Sometimes, amid such dire circumstances, we reporters protect ourselves by detaching. That's what I meant when I said earlier that we could appear blunt and insensitive at times. You know what I mean: A correspondent arrives at the scene of a bloody killing spree and asks a grieving mother how she feels about her loss. As you grow in experience and awareness, you realize that you know the answer to those kinds of questions already.

Your most difficult moments make you a better person if you allow them to. By the time the South African AIDS assignment came along, my career was solid. I had received a couple of Emmys and was on a stellar team of storytellers at KSTP Channel 5 in Minneapolis. What I had learned by then was that the toughest parts of my journey so far had prepared me for covering this travesty. All of my prior assignments had revealed to me one of the most necessary ingredients for delivering award-winning journalism: *Integrity*. I never asked a dying eighteen-year-old African woman what it was like to leave her newborn behind in an orphanage run by Western nuns. But she told me everything anyway because I remained engaged and patient. Respect for integrity—hers, my own, and of those who were there to help—informed my every move. I did not rush her or assume anything about her. I also promised myself I'd visit an orphanage where children like hers were cared for and prayed over by a group of Christians. That visit haunts me to this day. I saw firsthand how being a person of integrity, honesty, and grace opens doors to possibility when it seems as if nothing else could. The term *behind-the-scenes* took on a new and far deeper meaning for me. I learned that integrity hides in the recesses of the most difficult choices and certainly in sacrifice. You may be tempted to look away at times. But don't. Integrity is the truth that ultimately surfaces beneath the pain. And it's a truth you will sometimes encounter *and* use in the most unexpected places.

Similarly, it was desire to exercise integrity that guided an unexpected choice in my coverage of the Natalee Holloway case. I was on assignment in Aruba for *A Current Affair* after Natalee had disappeared. I was in the lobby of the Holiday Inn when I saw her mother for the first time. She was staying at the hotel and it was apparent that she was desperately trying to find out all that she could about her daughter's whereabouts. It was just three days after Natalee went missing and she was full of questions herself.

It was clear she wouldn't have any answers for me. She was trying to get vital information from the medical authorities and from the other teens who were with her daughter on a trip to the Caribbean. There were no signs of reporters yet. Many were just booking their flights as the story was developing. I put myself in this mother's place and knew that I couldn't push for an interview yet. There are just some moments when you have to be human and trust that when the time is right you will still be able to pursue the story. Our professional relationship grew from that act of respect. Beth Holloway did take part in a half-hour special I did examining her daughter's disappearance some time after that. It was a decision I look back on now and still believe was the right choice.

For years, when I gave motivational talks to large groups of people, I frequently highlighted this rule about putting integrity first. It seemed as if talking about the concept of doing the right thing was another way to uphold and spread the value to others. I told audiences that it makes you stand out from the crowd in the best of ways. I explained that integrity is at the crux of great leadership. It is how you impel and inspire others to follow you. I assured them that people look for goodness all the time. It is hard to resist the magnetism of someone who is fair and steady in applying the right principles to the right actions. It was a perfect topic for corporations looking to cultivate quality employees.

I also talked about how certain moments will test you and reveal whether you possess integrity to the extent it is needed. I reminded listeners that integrity means you are the same person whether you win or lose. People with integrity expect excellence from themselves and others no matter what is happening around them. Whether the outcome of an effort is good or bad, they exhibit unwavering respect for others, and maintain the ability to assess their own, their underlings', and their competitors' performances objectively. Integrity involves learning from failure and pressing on, as that is how you get through each battle, from one to the next.

I knew these words were needed because there is so much emphasis in our society on doing well instead of doing good. But I didn't know the full extent to which they were necessary until the world was rocked by sexual harassment scandal after sexual harassment scandal over the course of the last year—including in my own place of work. Industry after industry purged predators from their midst who were abusing their power. No one was too big to oust. It was as if we were collectively releasing a torrent of integrity and clearing a path for new leadership to emerge. People are learning to say something when they see something—not just in the war on terror, but in the one on individual rights.

For those who are concerned that they did not do enough in cases that were *open secrets* or in situations where someone confided their circumstances, it is never too late to learn from these experiences. Integrity is activated by choice and you can choose to use it from this point forward whenever it is needed.

The same advice applies to those who noticed and failed to take action to stop the bad actors in the military who committed sexual harassment and assault offenses against fellow troops.

In preparation for writing this chapter I wanted to know more about how the military currently instills integrity in its enlisted men and women, so I reached out to Democratic Congresswoman Tulsi Gabbard to find out. A few years ago, at the White House Correspondents' Dinner, she was seated at my Fox News table and we had a chance to get acquainted. For those of you who may not know this about her, in addition to representing the state of

Hawaii in Congress, she is also a major in the Hawaii Army National Guard, which means that she is both a US legislator and an active military officer at the same time. Now that's what you call doing double duty for your country.

I thought that given her ongoing service, her views on the subject of integrity could add value to this chapter. The conversation ultimately made its way toward the challenges the military faces to halt harassment, but before it did I was happy that she provided some wonderful examples of how the vast majority of troops still possess integrity and act on this core tenet.

As we began talking, she told me that she was really impacted by 9/11 and that, like so many other people across the country who recognized what we lost in those attacks, she wanted to do her part to serve. She was actually a member of the Hawaii State Legislature when she enlisted. She took the oath of office on the floor of the state house of representatives and soon thereafter, when their legislative session was done for that year, shipped off to Fort Jackson, South Carolina, for basic training. Shortly after her return home, Hawaii's 29th Brigade Combat Team was activated for a year-long deployment to Iraq, but she was not on the mandatory deployment roster. However, she knew that she could not stay home and watch her fellow soldiers go into combat, so she left what looked to be an easy reelection campaign and volunteered to deploy with her Hawaii soldiers to the Middle East not once but twice. Right there I recognized one of the most common signs of integrity that *all* of our military service members exhibit. Feeling called to defend our country, to protect the principles it upholds, and to respond to that calling by signing up is surely one of the clearest reflections of integrity, whether it is during a time when we are actively engaged in war, when conflict is imminent, or when we are at peace and only the prospect of being deployed someday to unknown places under unknown circumstances exists.

From there she explained that when she enlisted in the Army, all soldiers were handed a yellow and white plastic card no bigger than a business card. They had to carry this with them at all times. Written on it were all the values the Army expects of you, including integrity. She told me how these values were inculcated into soldiers every single day of training. At all the different ranges where they trained, there were little vignettes posted about soldiers who served in previous conflicts and were killed in the line of duty. Each story addressed how these soldiers embodied a different Army value, whether it was integrity, honor, selfless service, personal courage, or one of the others, such as loyalty, duty, and respect. So every single day on multiple occasions troops learned not only about what these values mean, but they learned how important they are in our service and in our everyday lives. She stressed something I mentioned earlier as well:

"It doesn't matter whether someone is watching you or not," she said. "When you take that oath of office to protect and defend our constitution and our country you are making a choice—not for a nine-to-five job but for a lifestyle. It is clear to you that you no longer represent only yourself; you represent your country. So the responsibility of maintaining that integrity, of standing with that integrity, of living with that integrity is about something much bigger than just yourself, or your own interests, or your own future. Especially when your decisions can literally be the difference between life and death."

She also talked about how integrity is more than just taught in the Military Academy and in Officer Candidate School (OCS): It is consciously tested and reinforced as well. "You can literally get

kicked out of Officer Candidate School for an honor code violation," she told me. "If you lie, if you say something that isn't true,
if you violate your own integrity, then you get expelled."

Of course, this process involves a fair hearing. She explained
that when you are suspected of a violation, you sit in front of an
honor board, which includes your superiors as well as someone
who is your peer. You can make your case and tell your story.
Evidence is provided on both sides. The consequences for being
found guilty are serious. If you are released from Officer Candidate School because of an honor code violation then you will not
serve as a commissioned officer in the US military by any means.

I asked her if she ever witnessed this process and she told me
that she had. A few years after she attended Officer Candidate
School in Alabama, she returned there to serve as a TAC Officer,
which is very much like a drill instructor. (TAC is an acronym
for Train, Assess, Counsel.) During that time she helped train
hundreds of officer candidates, one of whom was investigated for
such an honor code violation during training. This candidate's
Operations Orders were so well done that some of his instructors
questioned whether they had been plagiarized or copied from another source. She was asked to weigh in on whether or not he had
cheated, because he had been prepped for OCS by some of the
same officers who prepped her before she went through training.
After scrutinizing the facts of the case and his work, knowing full
well the rigors and the high caliber of his prep training, she was
convinced that he hadn't plagiarized, but rather due to his training, he executed the task very well, exceeding the standard. If he
had been found guilty of the charges, however, he would have
been kicked out. Fortunately, that wasn't the case and he serves as
a captain and company commander in the Army to this day. But

the point here is that the military wants its troops to understand that there are consequences for not acting with integrity at all times. As Congresswoman Gabbard says, "Once you compromise your integrity, once you compromise yourself, there's no coming back from that."

When we made our way to the topic of sexual assault in the military, we found a direct link to what integrity and those Army values mean when dealing with difficult challenges, both as soldiers and as leaders. According to her there are two ways to go about things. "One way is to be honest and to have integrity when dealing with the shortcomings at hand, whatever they may be. That involves calling on your strength and courage to actually solve the problem. The other path is to hunker down, sweep the issue under the rug, and 'protect your own' out of fear of exposing your shortcomings. Frankly, the latter is a disservice to our troops, our military, and to our country. The example of sexual assault in the military is an important one; it's also a complex one where oftentimes people have a mistaken sense of loyalty to their units or to their friends, so they cover up or deny that instances like these occur at all. Rather than dealing with the issue, soldiers are reassigned somewhere else where everyone hopes the problem will just go away. It doesn't. That doesn't solve anything, nor does it serve the best interests of our troops or our nation. Instead, we must recognize that real loyalty to one's troops, to our military, and to the country involves choosing the hard right path over the easy wrong path. You have to actually address the problem head-on, even if it may mean you have to discipline someone that is a friend or who you may be close to."

As we closed the conversation it was evident to me that the issue of integrity has never been more important in both our military and in our civilian population. It is heartening to see the different ways these values are being demanded by the public and instilled and reinforced in the more aware and responsive parts of our culture, but it must permeate all of our society, and that means it is up to each of us to individually live by this rule. I am deeply committed to keeping it a topic of conversation at my speaking engagements and to acting on it in my own life. Collective mindfulness on the subject is how we guarantee our own and our country's excellence.

BEING TRUE TO YOURSELF

Think about the vignettes Congresswoman Gabbard talked about. The military reinforces core values through personal stories. Collect the stories of people you admire. Seeing how they act with integrity will give you ideas about how you can do the same. What I'm hoping you will discover is that integrity is not in as short a supply as we fear—and that in some cases, it may be underutilized, but it is there below the surface ready to be activated.

So begin by asking yourself the following questions:

Are there people in your life whose stories inspire you? Look to your family, friends, teachers, community members, former or present bosses, mentors, and colleagues first. How do they best exemplify integrity?

By the way, as you compile this list, don't be surprised to find some overlap with those who are your special forces or those who are in your inner circle. I assume you have chosen these friends because they are people of their word. But try to also think of examples even beyond that level of closeness to you as well. It will give you greater confidence that there are others out there seeking to live or actually living according to these same high values.

Think about the actions of the people on your list. How have they handled both success and failure? Do they own their mistakes and set out to correct them or at least bear them in mind for the next time?

How could you join forces with these people? How can you interact with them more? Or follow their lead? Can you invite them to do things with you socially? Are they willing to meet with you for coffee to talk about how they developed this quality in themselves? Come prepared with questions, especially if there are challenges you are facing where you don't know how to exert your integrity. They may be able to help you think through a solution. Remember: We are most like the people we spend the greatest amount of time with.

Now broaden the compilation of stories to include people in history whom you believe possessed integrity. After you have added them to your list, ask yourself if there is anyone in society today who displays this quality? Your inspiration can come from *any* field of endeavor. For example, they can hail from entertainment, politics, media, the art world, or industry, to name a few areas.

How do they express their integrity?

Because you cannot keep their company in the same way you can with people you know personally, how else can you learn from them? Are there books or blogs they've written that you can read? Do they conduct speaking engagements or workshops you can attend? Can you follow some of them on social media? Remember, by choosing to follow them, you are signaling your approval of the way they conduct themselves. When you like the posts of those who model integrity, you are supporting both their work and their values. Don't throw your likes away on people who are not deserving.

I've told you how I define integrity, and now you also have examples of how others define it. But how do you define it? Do you have a moral code that you consciously or unconsciously try to live by? Whether your answer is yes or no, write up a personal code of conduct you'd like to live by now. It's good to have one handy. It should include the attributes and behaviors that you think define a person with integrity. The military has such a code. You should too.

Since integrity begins with truth, be honest with yourself. What qualities about you are you most proud of? How many of them are on the list you just made? How many of them are qualities you have in common with the people in the stories you've collected? Which attributes on the list are you missing and what behaviors do you think you still need to work on?

Know that integrity and accountability go hand in hand. One at a time, pick a quality on the list you made and find ways to express it in your everyday life. If honesty is one of those qualities, for example, determine to be truthful in all of your interactions. That means no stretching the facts for effect or to make you look better in a situation at work or in a relationship. It also means no blaming anyone else when something goes wrong, especially if you contributed to the problem. None of us is infallible—even people with tons of integrity—so if you do behave in a way that is not aligned with the list you've made, own the action and try as best you can to correct it.

There are times when integrity will require that you make some really tough decisions, but to condition yourself to do that you first have to practice living with integrity in daily and more achievable ways. Do you keep your promises to others? Or do you frequently change plans? Do you say what you are thinking or do you say what you think others may want to hear? Do you take shortcuts or do you take care and time to complete a task well? Do you take risks or do you shy away from them even when it means something you value is at stake?

A good way to monitor the integrity of your actions is to consider how the people you love most in the world might react if they knew what you were about to do or not do. This was a tact my father used when he reminded those service members under his command to consider what their mothers would think before they engaged in vices that threatened their safety.

There may be times when you will enter a gray area where the pros and cons of acting one way or another are not clear—and times when there are consequences for a right choice just as there are for a wrong choice. When we talk about accountability, some people can feel trapped because they are bound to someone contractually or financially who does not share their moral code. Integrity dictates that your accountability lies with your conscience first. I understand that this is not an easy reality but neither is the alternative. My hope is that as more of us act with integrity we won't be put in positions where we feel we must compromise ourselves and our values.

You have the right intentions, you are armed with some great examples of how others have faced the same challenges, and you have surrounded yourself with people who can help you in this regard in the event you need help. Now go nurture, practice, and unleash your integrity on the world!

Rule #7

THINK LIKE A GENERAL

One of my father's greatest aspirations for himself, those he loves, and certainly those he commanded during his military career was for each of us to be good leaders. By that he doesn't necessarily mean that we should all be bosses or we should seek to be the only power in a situation. He raised me to understand that leadership means being an individual who sets a good example. Someone who learns from what has happened in history and who is highly attuned to what is happening in the present. Leaders take a measure of their surroundings and of events beyond those surroundings, making informed choices with that knowledge. They plan and intend for those choices to benefit their team and others seeking the same goals. When one is really exemplary, that leader's presence is felt even though he or she may not be standing right next to you. Leadership has to do with imprinting who you are on others so they can follow suit when the time comes for them to make wise choices too.

My father was inspired by many wonderful leaders through-out his career. He encountered some while in the field and had the occasion to meet others during his time at the Pentagon. A particularly proud moment for him was meeting General French of the VII Corps. The general paid my dad an eagerly received compliment during a chance meeting one day. My father was getting ready to return to Vietnam on assignment when French stopped him and asked, "Are you the Signal Corps operations officer?" My dad replied, "Yes," and told the general that he had also done some work for the Civil Corps division. French said, "We have never had communications like this before. Keep up the good work." My father thanked him, told him he was on his way back to Vietnam, and saluted him before boarding his wait-ing plane. My father was stationed for twenty-three months in Stuttgart, Germany, between his two tours of duty in Vietnam. As an example of the kinds of strides he made for the Corps there, he once caught some serious errors in the placement of signals on a collapsed bridge near a major waterway during a practice maneuver that could have proven catastrophic if those signals had been positioned that way in a live combat situation. When he pointed the errors out and acted quickly to rectify the problem, he impressed the higher-ups. The wrong placement had either escaped the notice of those running the exercises or was not thought through correctly. While the general was not present for the exercise, it was comfort and encouragement for my dad to know that the general was receiving reports and that corrections in the field could be relayed and made so none of our troops would be endangered by our Signal Corps' own omissions or errors. My father has said at that time the VII Corps group was as good a general's group as he'd ever known because the general was a very hands-on kind of person. He knew the performance of his major units for sure.

My father also admired one of his contemporaries: Colin Powell, whom we all know went on to become a four-star general, the twelfth chairman of the Joint Chiefs of Staff, secretary of state, and an overall statesman. As my father has said, "It was the perception of everyone around him that General Powell would never go into a situation undermanned. He carefully assessed what he needed and secured the resources that would best support his people and his mission. He is someone who understood force-structure. He honed in on the demands of whatever region or terrain we were in at the time, and assembled the best assets for the operation. Then he maintained that force structure in such a way as to keep it primed and ready for use whenever it was needed." My father respected him for this and much more.

GENERALLY SPEAKING

Every amazing parent I know hopes to raise their children to make good decisions in their absence. Imprinting them with the capability to do this is true leadership. All the great bosses I've worked for have also wanted to impart wisdom to their staff for the same reason—so that we would make smart choices when they weren't around or when they delegated responsibility to us. Imprinting our employees with the capability to do this is also true leadership. Thinking like a general—aka modeling successful behavior—is on my list of rules to live by because sometimes, when we are faced with challenges, we need to look around and draw from the examples of others even more practiced at being successful than we are. These people are the generals in our lives. We are all lucky to have them in our midst, but we also must remember that we are each capable of being a general ourselves.

TAKING CHARGE

When I was seven years old I rode around all of Fort Leavenworth on my purple bicycle. I still needed training wheels and an adult at my side, but good luck trying to keep up with me! My teddy bear Jennie sat in the front basket as we made our way past the museum, the chapels, and the vast burial grounds—one of the twelve original national cemeteries established by Abraham Lincoln in 1862. More than thirty thousand veterans and their loved ones are buried there. Among them are Captain Thomas Ward Custer—a double Congressional Medal of Honor recipient—and Major General Edward Hatch, an officer with the Union Army during the Civil War who later became the first commander of the 9th US Cavalry Regiment. As some of you history buffs may know, that was the first regiment of black enlisted men. The second such regiment, the 10th Cavalry, was constituted at Leavenworth in 1866. In that big cemetery you can also find the oldest known US military grave, that of Captain James Allen, of the 1st US Dragoons. And, of course, after some movement, the remains of Brigadier General Henry Leavenworth, the fort's namesake, have been laid to rest there as well.

The place is steeped in history and is the ideal setting to groom promising young men and women into future top military brass. In fact, we were stationed in Leavenworth, Kansas, because my father was one of those future leaders studying at the US Army

Command and General Staff College, originally known as the School of Application for Infantry and Cavalry when it was established by General William T. Sherman in 1881. Among the school's many famous graduates were General Dwight D. Eisenhower and General George S. Patton.

It was common for me to see high-ranking officers being driven around in jeeps during the day and just as common for me to hear my dad talking about the traits that distinguished them from others at our dinner table each night. My father would say every great general knows the job and role of each rank he leads. That's how he gains their respect. He looks them in the eye and says, "I get you," and he means it. It's why when he then says, "Now go follow my orders," they do.

My dad would also tell my mother and me, "Generals like accountability. They don't shrink from it." One of the generals he taught me about was Henry Leavenworth, the man who not only built our post, but several others throughout the western United States. He was known for having led infantrymen into decisive battles in the War of 1812 and beyond.

Recalling these mealtime lessons led me in more recent years to enjoy reading about different military leaders and to speak about them when I give motivational talks to the public or to employees of large corporations. I now tell audiences that generals such as Leavenworth knew that our biggest advantage in almost every situation is to have a weapon no one can see—a toughness of mind that the enemy cannot track or predict. Such generals are able to spot the strength of their own forces and delegate accordingly so their time and energy is better spent strategizing. They are aware that, over time, stress and emotional drama weakens one's ability to focus and win, so they remove those obstacles from their lives as best they can. In more current terms, I tell audiences that thinking like a general is all about protecting your personal bandwidth—your brain and your physical energy combined. This is important because generals need to learn more than they think they will ever have to know, so that extra knowledge gives them an edge over their adversaries when the time arises.

It was during dinners at Fort Leavenworth and while riding around its beautiful grounds, soaking in all the lore about our military leaders, that this rule first took shape. My parents' words and actions, coupled with these warriors' stories, had imprinted the value of being a leader on me and I knew it had to be distilled down into a message we could all remember.

LEADING BY EXAMPLE

When contemplating how to best illustrate examples of applied leadership in this chapter, I realized that I should probably *show* you rather than *tell* you how great generals think. So I invited one of the most impressive people I know to help me. General Jack Keane is a retired four-star general and former vice chief of staff of the United States Army. He was a key architect of the surge strategy that changed the way the United States fought the war in Iraq. He is also a national security strategist serving as chairman of the board at the Institute for the Study of War. Many of you know him as a media consultant and frequent contributor to Fox News, which is how I was fortunate enough to meet him. He graciously agreed to be interviewed for this book and I am grateful that he did. My seven-year-old self only imagined conversations with generals in her head. This talk was very real and was intended to focus on the ways lessons from his career could help you on your journey to success, whatever your field may be.

I was curious about when and why General Keane joined the Army, so that is where the conversation began.

"I came into the military at age twenty-three," he told me. "I really should have joined at twenty-one but it took me six years to get through Fordham University. My father passed away right after my sophomore year, so I had to leave twice and come back. Fordham staff wanted me to attend night school, but I found out I could only stay in ROTC if I was a day student. We were a working-class family, so I took classes whenever I could, held a part-time job initially, and then during my last two years, I worked 4:00 P.M. to midnight in the Wall Street area."

Knowing what I did about a leader's determined disposition, it didn't surprise me that General Keane marked his foray into service by overcoming obstacles. I also came to understand that core values were *imprinted* on him by family at a young age too.

He told me, "My father was a World War II marine and all the men in the family that I grew up with who were military-age served during the war. Every service was represented. No one had been an officer—or for that matter, no one was a college graduate. And no one had ever made it a career. But there was a powerful sense—and I don't think this was unique to them—of serving the country in times of need. To a person, they knew they had participated in something that was truly crucial to the country. There's never been an event like World War II in the history of mankind. One hundred million people were killed as a result of that experience in the Pacific and in the Atlantic. So it was something that defined the world at the time and the men in my family participated in it. It was something of a defining lifetime experience for many of those men. So not that we spent a lot of time talking about it, but there was always a prevalent attitude that encouraged doing what was right for the country."

What he said next was fascinating to me.

"I also had sixteen years of a Catholic education, culminating at Fordham, which is a Jesuit school. I often joke with my military friends—officers who are largely non-Catholic—that after sixteen years of Catholic education, the transition to the Army was a smooth one. While Fordham was an intellectual crucible, because it follows the rigorous Jesuit curriculum and methodology, there was always an undercurrent of service to others in that Jesuit experience, so I think that was a factor in terms of its impact on me as well.

"I was drawn to the military because the idea of serving the country had tremendous appeal to me, but I didn't know for certain whether I had the aptitude for it. Nobody truly does unless you submit yourself to it and find out. I also think that a military profession—if you are pursuing it—is kind of akin to a vocation, particularly for those who are in the fighting organizations, because the characteristics it demands are pretty similar to a vocation: Self-sacrifice, service to others, dedication, and discipline."

He paused, then continued.

"I always thought that serving America as a soldier most of my adult years really defined my life and helped develop the person that I became. I must add that I was also honored and humbled to spend a life among true heroes—people for whom death was always a silent companion."

I found this answer to be packed with so much meaning in the context of what we have already discussed in this book. Being mentally and spiritually ready enables us to physically take chances to meet our goals. I also think General Keane's answer reflects the fact that so many successful people think of the work they do as having a larger purpose in life.

Next, I decided to ask him about his decision-making process. All of us will be tasked with making important choices in our lifetime and since generals must do so under even more extreme conditions than we may ever face, I thought his insight could help guide us.

"Well, not too surprisingly," he said, "the decision-making process around challenging, complicated issues always involves tough choices because there are no easy options. Every option is fraught with something that is negative about it. All that said, you do the best that you can based on judgment and experience. But what I found every bit as important as the decision itself was that once I made the decision I never questioned it. I got behind it with all the force and passion of my personality and also with sheer leadership drive, so that the entire enterprise would indeed be committed.

"The reality is, once you make a decision, what you're really looking for is excellent execution. I found, at least in my experience, that execution is so crucial, it compensates at times for a less than satisfactory decision—or even for a decision that is off the mark."

I wanted to understand this better and knew you would want to as well, so I asked how he arrived at this strategy.

"My approach, I think, had more to do with who I am and with just learning from your mistakes," he explained. "I also found that in the decision-making process it's best not to procrastinate over the difficulty of the decision because it's not going to get any easier. The negative aspects of all the options are not really going to change very much. Particularly in the world that we're involved in with the military, if your staff or other commanders are bringing you options that are well thought out—and I'm assuming that they are—usually the sooner you make a decision, the better. The process does demand a degree of decisiveness. That allows the entire team—the organization—to be able to prepare, rehearse, and devote a large amount of their time to getting ready as opposed to devoting most of their time to just making the decision."

Because the general has worked outside of the military for a number of years now, I asked if he could tell us what skills or attributes a general possesses that could benefit a civilian striving for success in their career. It is a complicated question, so he responded with a few welcome answers.

"I think success begins with knowing yourself and being honest with yourself about your own limitations and weaknesses. That's where I would start.

"Second, you need to have absolute competence in your craft.

"And I think a third attribute is having passion for what you do because passion is very contagious and it can help motivate and inspire others."

He continued, "In the military what makes us different—not necessarily special, but different—is that the mission always comes first and we have to accomplish it despite the obstacles and the impediments that are present. So I find that there's another attribute that stands out among all others, as it applies to the military or a civilian profession: Perseverance.

"You know for us, no matter how challenging the mission is, we have to have the tough-mindedness to succeed even at the expense of our troops and ourselves. There is no second place. It truly is who we are. I will say that when I'm critical of other leaders it's usually because they don't persevere through all the obstacles and impediments. Perseverance is essential to succeed consistently."

While I was aware of the general's impeccable record, I wondered if there were any examples of wartime mistakes he felt he had made, and if so, how he dealt with those mistakes. I appreciated his forthright answer.

"Well, let me tell you about one where we were actually involved in combat," he began. "It's during the Vietnam War and I'm a platoon leader in what they call airborne infantry—a battalion from the 101st Airborne Division. So we were infantry paratroopers. And I have very good soldiers and very good sergeants. At times they were so brave I had to hold them back so that we wouldn't overextend ourselves. But nonetheless, I'm in this unit x number of weeks—I forget exactly how long but it was several weeks—and my routine would be to try to ambush as many nights as I possibly could in a seven-day week. In other words, we would lay in wait for the enemy to come down a trail and we would ambush that enemy at night. We'd surprise them. We had a couple of successes in those weeks. Most of the time you stay there and nobody comes so you have to have the discipline to continue to do this. But one night when the enemy did come, we had an awful experience. While we took the enemy by surprise, myself and a couple of leaders were in what we call the kill zone—where the enemy soldiers are now laying—when all of a sudden a grenade went off. I thought initially that it came from the enemy—that they were coming to reinforce the soldiers that we had just fought. But it turned out it was from one of my soldiers who was providing rear security for the ambush position—a soldier who was farther back from where we were. It was absolutely inexplicable that something like that could happen.

It wounded a couple of my soldiers, who required medical evacuation. Because that was unacceptable to me, I told my commanders that I was going to train on this for a week."

I had never heard of such a thing, so I stopped him mid-answer. "How could you do this while you were still in the field?" I asked.

"Well, that's exactly what they wanted to know. They said, 'What do you mean *train*?' I said, 'I'm going to find a spot and I'm going to simulate a situation where the enemy is there and I'm going to actually conduct live fire exercises like I would do back at Fort Bragg or some other military base.' They asked, 'You're going to do that in a combat zone?' And I said, 'Yes, I'm going to do that in a combat zone.' I told them that after we did that, I would not stay there because we would have given our positions away. So I practiced that for a week and then I ambushed for twenty-six straight nights after that practice with considerable improvement and success. I learned something in doing that—in having the perseverance to really get it right."

My natural follow-up was: "What drives that kind of perfectionism?"

"When you're leading people in combat you can't help but feel the responsibility—the accountability—you have for their lives," he told me. "And you know full well that they're depending on you to get it right for them. Getting it right is making sure they're properly prepared. If the preparation is right, usually the execution is right. And that execution wasn't right because the preparation wasn't right. So that's what I fixed. And I think it helped me with so many other things that challenged me."

With a show of leadership like that I couldn't help but ask if the general thought leaders are born or made.

"I think both answers are correct," he said. "There are some natural-born leaders, but for most of us it's a journey of continued growth and development. I was in a leadership laboratory my whole professional life, spanning over forty years including the pre-commissioning experience. It began in ROTC with learning how to lead your peers. Then it continued as a platoon leader of forty, a company commander of one hundred and fifty, a battalion commander of seven hundred, a brigade commander of five thousand, a division commander of twenty thousand, a corps commander of ninety-six thousand, and then as a four-star general, an army of more than a million troops. That's an extraordinary journey where the entire experience is so much about your own personal growth and development as a leader. And I was sharing all those experiences with other leaders who were my peers, my superiors, and my subordinates, as I was learning so much from all of them."

Given all of this growth and development, I was intrigued to know if the general thought that joining the military changed his life trajectory. And if so, how? As with all of the other answers, he responded thoughtfully.

"Well, joining the military profession strengthened the values that I received from my parents and also from my Catholic education experience. Despite the fact that I was in the business school, one of my favorite courses at the university was philosophy. We not only had to minor in that subject but we had to wear black robes to those classes too. By way of explanation, my first Jesuit teacher said, 'When you come to an intellectual banquet, you come properly attired.' We were, after all, studying the great philosophers such as St. Thomas Aquinas. But what you're really doing when you study philosophy is exploring the meaning of life in its most profound understanding of it. We also had to take four years of theology. And, trust me, there was nothing rote about it. But those two courses together were incredibly thought provoking. They expanded my understanding of life. I only mention it in this context because when I got in the Army and I was exposed to war and what that truly means, I found it to be the most human of all experiences. All of your senses, in terms of what is happening to you as a human being, are so raw and so intense as a person—at least they were for me—that it gave me such an appreciation for the meaning and value of life. I intellectualized all of that in my Jesuit educational experience and then I went out and lived it with such intensity and passion in my everyday life. I don't know—I can't say what it would have been like if I was doing something else, because obviously I didn't do something else, but I think the military had a profound impact on who I am, and on my Terry and our kids as well."

With the mention of his wife and children, I wondered how the military affected the general's life in other ways, so I asked that too. His answer stirred memories of the dedication I saw run in whole military families, especially in some of the wives who were leaders themselves.

"Well, serving in the military for as long as I did was a defining life experience. I truly loved getting up every day to do it and I felt absolutely blessed to share that entire experience with my wife, Terry, who I married in college. We were able to raise two children who shared in the experience as well.

"It's very difficult, I think, to meet the sacrifices that a military profession demands of a family if the two adults in the family are not almost equally committed to the life. I was absolutely blessed because Terry loved army life every bit as much as I did. It was her life too. She was extraordinarily devoted to our soldiers, their families, and their welfare. You know, the army really got two people for the price of one because from the time I was a battalion commander— a lieutenant colonel at around thirty-eight years of age—she was intimately involved in helping the organization be better. And then when she became a general officer's wife, as I commanded a major organization, every day her calendar was chock-full of meetings and experiences. She was actively involved with all the functions on military bases that touched the lives of our families, the soldiers, and us. An officer's wife didn't have to do that. Some didn't want to do that, and that is okay. And it certainly wasn't easy, especially when you have to move as much as the Army can require you to do. We moved twenty-seven times and she was in charge of it all! And not only that, she shared the same enthusiasm for it. We always, always looked forward to the next assignment."

I was already amazed by their dedication when the general recalled one more detail about his time in the armed services that really impressed me. I don't know many other people who could make this same claim. He said, "Terry was the only person who knew this, but when I retired and I had to make a speech, I was looking for a way to convince the people in the audience and the troops on the parade field of how much I was committed to military life, how much passion I had for them, and how much love I had for the experience. I told them the truth: That in all my thirty-eight years I never called in sick—not once. I had a good immune system to be sure, but I also loved getting up every day and getting the job done. Obviously, there were times when I wasn't feeling that well, but the draw to what I was doing was more powerful than staying at home and attending to myself. That attendance record epitomized how strong my feelings were about the life I was leading."

The commitment level General Keane exhibited is extraordinary. I mean, think about it: How many days of work have you missed over the course of your career? It led me to ask if he suspected generals tend to think similarly or differently than many of the leaders in industry, politics, and other pursuits outside of the military.

He paused for a moment and said, "That's an interesting question. Let me just answer it this way. Since I retired I've spent a considerable amount of time with leaders in other professions—people in the fields of business, education, medicine, and science. What I've observed is that the leaders in those professions have similar challenges to what I experienced. You know, they have to cope with crisis; they are challenged by organizational effectiveness; they have to try to build a competent team; they invariably get involved in very difficult personnel decisions. All of those are things that I have dealt with on a regular basis. The one difference, however, is that the stakes are higher in the military profession in terms of protecting the American people and the national interest. While leaders in other professions also fight to preserve life—they're certainly doing that in the medical profession—one of our most challenging human experiences in the military profession is the obligation to take lives, and at times in large numbers. This is such a demanding human experience that it requires strong values and a sound moral underpinning that are so central to our American democracy. I think to bear that challenge and to execute it properly can only be done when you actually and ironically have respect for human life. What I'm trying to say is that most of this is not all that different; many organizations have similar characteristics. What we all do is build effective teams. But the nature of our work in the military does separate us from all other professions. It doesn't make us any more special, but it is different."

We had time for only one more question, so I asked the general what he thought was missing in the lives of American people today that a military perspective could help with?

"First of all, it's important to note that the military is a microcosm of America. I mean we are racially, religiously, culturally, economically, and geographically diverse, but for us to be effective, we have to build strong unit cohesion," he told me. "We have to make certain that our teams are very capable. To do that, every single member of the team has to submit to something larger than self. That's the military's key to success. Despite all the differences that we may have, the only way we can succeed as a military organization is to be bound to each other. Our concern for each other has to trump our concern for ourselves. The team and its performance are more important than ourselves."

Just as I was about to ask for an example, he offered one.

"You know, I was watching the president speak before the American legion the other day when he brought this recipient of the Medal of Honor with him onstage. This man did something that few others have done before him. He threw himself on a grenade to save his teammates. He happened to survive it. Most don't. But that act is an example of the kind of commitment to others we try to create in our organization. It's not that to be in a military organization you have to perform such enormous feats of courage. No, that's not true at all. In fact, we don't think we're capable of achieving that. People who do this kind of thing are extraordinary. Nonetheless, an act like that captures and exemplifies what we're trying to achieve. So here a grenade is tossed at this man's team and he throws himself instinctively on that grenade without considering the consequences because he knows the team is likely to survive as a result of his action. He doesn't know whether he's going to survive or not, but he knows the team will. And that's the ultimate in terms of unit cohesion and submitting to something larger than oneself. This ideal is crucial to us.

"The other thing I want to say is that the only way you can get people who are as diverse as our folks in the military to perform to such a high standard is to eventually have enormous respect for each other and to actually appreciate the differences. And there's another thing that goes on that we never really talk about, but all of us who've lived it from time to time know it's there: There's a lot of love in these organizations. Most of these alpha males are not going to talk about that. Our alpha females are kind of the same way so that discussion is not going to happen. But it's there."

I certainly can attest to what the general was saying here. As a brat, I witnessed the kind of deep bonds that formed between service members and certainly between our families.

"What I see happening in America though is that there's a growing lack of respect and civility for each other, which translates into how we're treating each other," he continued. "People in the military don't act like that. If they do, they're not going to stay very long. We're going to try to find ways to bring them around if we can, or we will get rid of them. I mean, if we have a bigot on our hands, which we really don't get much of anymore— but if we do and we can't bring that person around—that person's going to be separated from the military. With some people, you know, it's always about themselves—constantly. Those people are so detrimental to our organization that even though they may have mental capacity or some other strong skill sets, if their attitude or behavior doesn't change, we'll get rid of them. We won't give them a dishonorable discharge or anything like that, but we will separate them because it's so important to us. So I think one of the things happening in America is we seem to respect each other less. We seem to be more uncivil. We seem to be emphasizing our differences in our country more, becoming less tolerant of those differences. That's something that would destroy a military organization and I do think it is weakening America as a nation."

As hard a truth as that may be to hear, General Keane's answer to this question is a call to action to ensure our society's continued success as well as our own. The rules in this book are a similar call to action.

I'm grateful for the opportunity to have spoken with the general. The history of leadership is more than facts and dates; it's personal stories of confidence and perseverance, inspiration, training, readiness, sound strategy, wise allocation of resources, and facing failure as responsibly as victory. General Keane has endured some of the same life challenges as the rest of us—and then some, for sure. His observations along the way prove that leadership is not a destination; it's a process. It's living life as an example, like the child who chooses to be a peacemaker instead of a bully in the schoolyard or the worker who chooses to be a change-maker instead of a critic. In time, those who make choices with forethought and integrity will find themselves in a position of power, motivating others to collectively strive toward the achievement of important goals. They will make mistakes. They will win and they will lose. They will lead some on missions who will flourish under their guidance and they will be saddened to see others fall by the wayside because of these others' own unattended demons. But with steady and determined effort, they will continue to grow, develop, and evolve as leaders. *You* can continue to grow and evolve as leaders.

EARNING YOUR STRIPES AND STARS

It takes years of experience and education to truly think like the best leaders in our armed services, but I'm certain that General Keane's words and a few of the following exercises will get you started.

Take a moment to assess your responses to various situations. Are you someone who stands back for a second to look at the bigger picture? Do you gather the facts before acting? Or are you someone who rushes in impulsively and thinks about the repercussions of that action later?

The best generals are several steps ahead of events—and certainly of their enemy—because they are observant at all times and think through possibilities in advance, so whatever actions they take are premeditated.

Practice your observation skills whenever you enter a room, a new situation, and even places you have been many, many times before. You will be surprised at how much you miss in your own environment day to day. Do this on an ongoing basis to sharpen this skill. And heed all the advice given in the rule "Wear Camo." Recon is a reflex action for most generals and knowing the best strategy to bring to wherever they may be is their strong suit.

When you face a challenge, what is your usual mode of attack? Do you remember the rule "Devise Your Mission"? Do you just cry, "War!" or do you enter the theater with a calculated, well-drawn plan that you are prepared and committed to execute with everything you've got?

By the way, how much have you considered diplomacy? Or the element of surprise? Your plan should have taken into account all the options in advance including plan Bs.

How well do you know your own weaknesses and strengths? Before you delegate anything, also be aware of the weaknesses and strength of those you are relying on for help. How ready and practiced are the special forces you recruited into your life after reading Rule #1? Remember to learn everything you can about your support team, including what they need from you in order to succeed. Then spend your every waking hour growing, developing, and learning more. When you and your forces train mentally, physically, and spiritually for all possible events, then you are more apt to be ready for the unforeseen ones too.

Does all of this sound familiar? It should. "Think Like a General" involves all the tenets of this book, including those not recapped here.

One final word on the subject: Paola Harrell told me about a time when her husband was concerned about his next promotion. He had been working toward his third star and he didn't know when or if it would happen. She was attending an event one evening with him when they saw a four-star general they hadn't seen in a while. His name was General William Livsey. He was someone the Harrells had admired for a long time and were grateful to for his support during Ernest's career. When this general sat down next to Paola at that event, he made a dollar bet with her that Ernest would indeed get his promotion. He knew the capabilities of her husband from the first time he met Ernest at Fort Benning.

That was where Ernest had his battalion command. Even though General Livsey had assumed responsibilities in Korea since that time—he was commander in chief of the United Nations Command, commander in chief of the ROK-United States Combined Forces, and commander general of the Eighth United States Army— he still kept an eye on Ernest from afar. The evening of that dollar bet, the general asked, "Are you worried too, Paola?" She said, "Yes, I am." Then he told her, "Look at my shoulders. What do you see?" She replied, "Four stars." He then said in a reassuring way, "Generals make generals." He was good to his word. Ernest was promoted shortly thereafter and didn't disappoint his mentor either.

Bear this story in mind when you succeed. As you are working to be the best leader possible, be sure to bring others who are leaders up along with you. It's what generals do. Generals make generals.

Rule #8

OWN YOUR MOMENT

There comes a time after a long pursuit of a goal, when you can finally reflect on and appreciate what you have accomplished. Sometimes it is publicly celebrated; other times it is more privately contemplated. My father told me that after he graduated from flight school he thought to himself, "If for no one else, this memory will be with me forever. I will be proud of it for all my days."

I gave you a sense earlier of what some military pilots go through to earn their wings, and of the difficult skills they must master in order to be able to pull off dangerous assignment after dangerous assignment, so you can imagine why those feelings welled up in him. He also felt that way after he accepted his Army commission. "There were just so many of us in my school and I was the only engineer," he explained. Engineers, of course, were among the most sought-after graduates in the military.

Understandably, there were times when processing a moment

before he tucked it away and moved on didn't come quite as easily to him. He once confided, "When I left my unit in Vietnam for the first time, I didn't understand how to do it. I wanted to hug every guy there, though it wasn't possible." How do you not become so completely overwhelmed by the gratitude you feel for your very survival together? I don't think I would have known a way to do that either.

There is a reason that the military has a deep history and elaborate customs surrounding the awarding of promotions and the public presentation of medals. Insignias do more than just reflect rank, for instance. They indicate and honor the level of responsibility and accountability the wearer bears. Moving up warrants a show of respect. It's a really big deal.

Medals, ribbons, and badges help acknowledge, communicate, and celebrate merit, honor, bravery, service, and sacrifice. They enable recipients to grasp and cope with the enormity of what they have accomplished and of what they've just been through. Decorations stir pride and confidence and they can sometimes heal what may have broken inside during the effort.

The military awards decorations for a wide range of achievements. There are *personal medals*. Perhaps the most well-known of these are the Medal of Honor, awarded for acts of valor; the Silver Star, awarded for gallantry in action; the Bronze Star, awarded for heroism in combat; and the Purple Heart, awarded for wounds suffered in combat. But there are also others for heroism outside of combat, extraordinary achievement in a particular discipline, and distinguished or meritorious service. There are *unit awards* including Presidential Unit Citations, Meritorious Unit Commendations, and Efficiency Awards. There are a host of *service awards* as well—from Prisoner of War, Good Conduct, Reserve, and Expeditionary medals to Special and General Service Awards. In addition, there are recruitment and training awards, guard ribbons, and professional development ribbons. And for sure, there are awards for *marksmanship*, too. My sincere apologies for any categories I may have missed, as the list is as exhaustive as the efforts of those who've earned such honors.

The point in telling you all of this is that there will be times certainly in the military and in life, when you will be called upon to reach beyond what you think you may be capable of doing. In those moments when you surprise yourself and you succeed, you may also be called upon to let others thank you in a more public setting. When this happens, I ask that you please, please, please stand up and be counted.

That may sound like an odd request from someone who writes about making decisions for no other reason than because it's the right thing to do, but sometimes accepting credit for your hard work *is* the right thing to do. It is not the time to be modest or the time to express your discomfort with formality. These commemorative events tell others that what seems impossible may not be impossible after all. And that is an important public service message, especially to those whose fears are totally justified in the face of war. In addition to being a symbol of bravery, you are also an example of perseverance and survival. I call the willingness and the act of receiving such honors with the requisite grace "owning your moment."

While my father didn't much like the fuss surrounding these ceremonies, he definitely understood the importance of them, and that motivated him to rise to the occasion.

Today he chooses to own the collective moments in his life by being an example to others in more interactive ways. Now that he is retired, he seeks out opportunities to connect with others who could gain something from his experiences in one-on-one conversations. For instance, when he was recently visiting a young cousin in Malakoff, Texas, he stopped off at the school he attended when he was a young boy growing up in that town. You will recall that while he felt he had received an excellent education from the four very dedicated teachers and the supportive school principal there, the facility was as tiny and grossly underfunded then as it is today. "Most graduates of that school feel as if they've come from nowhere," he told me. That is why he returns from time to time to give the current students the kind of heartfelt encouragement he received. He knows many of the students' parents, aunts, uncles, and grandparents from previous visits. He has been returning there on and off for years. The children will say, "I know you. You're that pilot. You're that engineer. You're that lieutenant colonel from the Army," and they also know that he was a graduate of that same school. The hope is that he will inspire at least one of them to see that goals are attainable even in difficult circumstances. He is really rooting for these kids, and hoping that they will have many occasions to own their moments in the future too.

PAYING IT FORWARD

Mentorship is such an important function in life. It inspires those coming up the ranks after us to grow and acquire the skills necessary to continue the work we've done when we move on to bigger challenges. Because our reach can't extend to all those looking for direction on a day-to-day basis, we must take advantage of recognition when it comes. It's important to share inspiring words and accumulated wisdom with the larger captive audience that gathers to celebrate our success with us. You never know how something you say will affect an eager listener or who that listener may someday become. They may be a general in the making or even a future commander in chief.

"Own Your Moment" is on my list because I do have occasion to speak publicly a lot and I know the impact other public speakers have made on me. Who has not been affected by a rousing TED Talk, graduation speech, or pep talk from a Hall of Famer accepting a lifetime achievement award? Gratitude for the opportunities afforded to you is best shown in the way you pass the ball, the baton, and your knowledge on to the next person.

A TEACHABLE MOMENT

I have vivid and magical memories of the battalion ceremonies my mother and I would attend when I was a little girl. We watched with pleasure as the various medals my father had earned were pinned to his uniform. My mother was as proud of the way my father would comport himself at these events as she was of the honors he was being given. She knew better than anyone that he did not like to be center stage. He's a very humble man. But he would carry himself with such poise in these situations because he knew what his predecessors' example had meant to him and he wanted to be a good example for those he commanded as well.

On the morning of these events my mother would remind him that if ever there was a time to stand up and own his moment, it was then. She used to say, "If you're going to rise, you may as well shine." When she was preparing me for the day and describing what would happen she would tell me that receiving acknowledgment for your accomplishments is an act of leadership. It's never self-congratulatory if you accept the honor in the right spirit. She would explain that it is vitally important for other people who aspire to do good work to see your efforts being appreciated and held up as something worth emulating. To shy away from this recognition is to somehow diminish the value of what you've achieved in the eyes of those looking on.

Mom also believed and told me it was part of the natural rhythm of success. Enjoying our moments in the spotlight enables us to stand down when it's time for others to shine. Once we've received our accolades, it's only fair to let others take center stage. When we're in sync with the ebb and flow of giving and receiving credit, there is never a reason to get jealous of other people who are advancing too. And that's extremely important, because jealousy is the opposite of integrity. Hearing the wisdom in these talks, my mantra regarding owning your moment became *Until the sun falls from the sky, we will have enough light to bask in and share.* Believe me, when people perform at their peak, it raises everyone so there is always enough adulation to go around.

You can see this practice embraced by the most admirable leaders. They know how to graciously accept credit, but they also know how to graciously give it. Paving the way for others to rise is the role they're meant to fulfill after they've shined for a while themselves. The highest achievers in society know they have further to go. They know that leadership is not the final destination. Every general I've ever met has been looking for that next step, even though it appears as if they are at the top of the stairway. They're determined to progress even if they have to create that next level

themselves. From the moment they've met their goals, they're looking for new challenges, wondering how their accumulated knowledge and experience could be put to even better use. They're also
looking behind them to see who could be pulled up from the ranks
to fill their present functions so the foundation they stand on in
their upcoming capacity will be as strong as the foundation they
upheld for their predecessors. That is how succession works. *Success*
is built into the word that describes this passing of the baton for a
reason. Both of the parties coming and going must have achieved
success for the transition to occur.

If you doubt for a moment that leadership is *not* a final destination, check out how many generals were up for cabinet positions during the early days of the Trump administration. We
haven't seen that many since the days of President Truman. Opportunities to utilize the diverse abilities, strengths, and integrity
of true leaders will always abound.

SHARING THE SPOTLIGHT

With my mother's words and these generals' examples in mind, I
try to leave room for my peers to shine around me too. Naturally,
I reach for as many opportunities to work as I can get. I do hours
and hours of programming each week because I love it. I'm addicted to breaking news and I focus on winning my time slot in
terms of ratings because that means I'm reaching more and more
people with the facts they need to know. I read everything I can.
I will invest every bit of energy I have to compete with the best of
the breaking news anchors out there, but as my executive produc-
ers have noticed and commented on, I also have a habit—which

I've consciously developed—of offering some of my air time so others can speak. I genuinely believe that people don't pause long enough on television to let others have their say.

The former copresident of our news division brought some marketing personnel down to the set of *Outnumbered* one day to observe us, and was shocked to hear me say to another panelist, "I'm going to yield my time to you." When he asked me why I did this, I explained that in some instances my moments of silence can further the conversation even more than speaking can. I won't interrupt or interject when someone else is saying something salient. If a question is put on the floor and I stop the flow of conversation to hear myself talk, where does the conversation go for the rest of the six-minute segment? I certainly take my time to say what I have to say, but I know the importance of giving others their due. I learned the good graces of listening from the leaders I observed growing up—leaders who knew how to share the spotlight. And I must say that this skill has secured many exclusive interviews for me over the years.

Some people, especially in a competitive environment, may think I'm being overly generous, but the truth is everyone gains from doing this, including me. It can open up all sorts of doors to extend mutual respect and sit quietly when other people around you have something to say. Listening is just as strong an attribute of a good communicator as speaking well is.

I also heeded my mother's advice to rise and shine on those occasions when I've been granted special recognition. I've been blessed to earn six Emmy Awards, including one for Best Newscaster and one for Best News Special in 2004, and I was bestowed with the Amelia Earhart Pioneering Lifetime Achievement Award for Humanitarian Efforts in 1998. On each of these occasions I tried to bear in mind the example of others who have impressed me with their dignity as they accepted praise.

A more recent moment that I especially enjoyed, and am grateful for, occurred during a spring 2017 event held by The Paley Center for Media to celebrate influential women in the television industry. Carol Burnett and Marlo Thomas were being honored and I couldn't have been more excited to meet them both. I was also thrilled to be listed as one of the celebrity guests on the invitation alongside many other women I admire. As was perfectly fitting for a night that was intended to commemorate the strength of the female voice, each special guest was asked to comment on what feminism means to her as she walked the red carpet. I love red-carpet moments in general because they present such a wonderful opportunity to uplift others, to focus attention on a particularly relevant issue or topic, and of course to embrace one's own career highlights. But this red-carpet walk somehow felt even more wonderful than most. When it was my turn to comment on what feminism means to me I said, "I want them [the upcoming generation of young girls] to feel the strides that women in my generation and previous generations have made for them. So you can label it whatever you want—I call it love."

It was so nice to have a chance to express this view. On a night when I was surrounded by so many who had done so much, I wanted to use the moment to give a nod to the pioneers while also cheering on the women of the future. When writers for the blog MAKERS.com reported on the event, I was glad to see that my comment resonated with others enough to become a featured quote and video clip. It was as if I got to enjoy that red-carpet moment all over again, and I was happy that others who weren't present got to hear my message too. My mother would have been very proud of me, I'm sure.

I not only use this rule whenever I can, I also tend to look for ways others apply it. You can never have enough inspiring examples of grace in the limelight to draw upon for later. I offer a few of my favorites below.

The Oprah Phenomenon

A lot of my understanding about ownership has come from observing megacommunicator Oprah Winfrey. No one owns a moment, aha or otherwise, like the queen of talk TV. Every minute she gave away a car to an audience member or connected with viewers over details of her abusive childhood, she owned it. Whether it is through her generosity, which became epic in TV history, or through her uncanny ability to join hearts and minds with her own, Oprah has found a way to imprint her brand onto any second in time as it is happening. Even when she makes mistakes they are like no one else's. I was watching when she stepped into hot water with the beef industry after making negative remarks on her talk show. Their retribution was swift. A group of angry cattle ranchers in Texas filed a $10.3 million lawsuit claiming she defamed the entire industry. They lost. On that day in 1998, she exclaimed to reporters as she walked out of the courthouse, "Free speech not only lives, it rocks." With her worldwide image at stake and literally on trial, she owned her moment by making it about free speech, something every American at the very least could grasp and in many cases support.

My favorite Oprah quote has to do with knowing when it's your time to shine. She has said, "When you were built to be tall, you will endanger your position if you lower your perspective. We eat on the level of our vision. Giraffes eat from the top of the trees. Turtles' view is from the ground."

Thanking My Lucky Stars!

While I have only watched Oprah own moments from afar, I did have a wonderful opportunity to personally witness another fine celebrity display the kind of leadership and graciousness I admire. It was at a Hollywood event not too long ago. It occurred at the 21st Century Fox New York City Premiere of the film *Hidden Figures*.

As many of you know, the National Board of Review named the movie one of the top ten of 2016. Certainly one reason why so many of us loved it is because the film, and the book it's based on, finally give long-overdue credit to three real-life exemplary African American women—former NASA mathematician Katherine Johnson, former NASA data supervisor Dorothy Vaughan, and former NASA engineer Mary Jackson—all of whom astronaut John Glenn and others have acknowledged were very instrumental in advancing the US space program during a crucial time in its history.

But we also loved the movie for the performances by its stellar cast—superstar Kevin Costner as well as actresses Taraji P. Henson, Octavia Spencer, and Janelle Monáe. At the after-party that evening, everyone naturally gushed over Costner. Who doesn't love him?! We could have listened to him talk for hours, but after obligingly and congenially answering a few of the crowd's questions, he quickly turned over the mantle to his costars by saying, "Enough about me. Why don't you ask what it was like to work with these fabulous women?" He has enjoyed being heralded by the media and by fans for so many years that at that particular moment he wanted to lift his costars up into the light instead. He recognized that each was a rising star and he wanted to be sure they were recognized as such. But even more than that he wanted them to bask in their moment. To enjoy the praise the film was receiving. They deserved it. Their performances were terrific. They brought their A-game to the film. It was a very special evening. I not only got to chat with Kevin Costner that night; I got to witness him invite others to rise and shine. That was an amazing moment!

A quick word on encouraging others to shine: The example above is the right way to do it. The moment is offered to those who have truly earned it. But increasingly in America, we are giving out awards to people just for participating in a challenge. This has certainly been the parenting trend of recent generations. Unfortunately, this doesn't teach anyone to earn his or her moment, let alone own it. It's a practice that breeds entitlement and undermines our goal-setting and goal-meeting capabilities as individuals and as a nation. It is also disappointing to see how often our culture elevates people who lack integrity or genuine achievement to celebrity status. If we fail to raise the bar high enough, over time we will certainly become less and less capable of achieving greatness. When we reserve these moments instead for people who truly deserve accolades, everyone's standards rise and what the honoree offers is not just inspiring words, but a history of action that serves as a blueprint for others to follow.

Giving Personal Thanks

As many times as the military proudly hosts events to salute its troops—and as many times as we may be honored publicly in our careers—there are also times when rewards come to us with far less fanfare. That does not make them any less meaningful. They need to be owned just like any other moment of honor. I was reminded of this point when both Congresswoman McSally and Congresswoman Gabbard recounted such moments with me.

Representative Gabbard told me about when she had been deployed to Kuwait as a platoon leader to fulfill a variety of different missions. In addition to running security patrol for shipments coming into the ports, providing safe escort for them up to the border of Iraq, and conducting a variety of goodwill visits with first responders, disabled children, and others in the host nations where she was stationed, she and a few others were individually tasked with providing training to the Kuwait Army National Guard. This included instructing them on everything from weapons training, marksmanship, and a whole host of other basic Army tasks and drills.

What made this particularly challenging was that *the Kuwaiti military doesn't allow women on their bases at all.* As Tulsi explained, "It doesn't matter if you're a janitor or if you're the Kuwaiti general's wife—no women allowed." So when she showed up on the first day of training in her US Army uniform, her hair pulled back tightly in a bun, the Kuwaiti gate guards seemed puzzled about what to do. They checked her ID, looked around at each other, and kind of shrugged, but ultimately they waved her through. Later, as she made her way down the line of the soldiers she and her team would be training, and as she put her hand out to meet them, half of them refused to shake her hand or look her in the eye. "I was invisible to them," she told me.

"It was as though I wasn't even standing there. But rather than screaming or yelling at them, I understood where they were coming from and went about my business. I had a job to do." In time, some of them started to notice that she knew how to shoot better than them. Some began to see that they could learn from her. As they got to know each other, she earned their respect. She worked with each of them until they all successfully completed their training. But what happened next was the kind of unantici-pated reward I'm talking about. She told me that on their gradu-ation day from this training course, their commander arrived and unexpectedly called her in front of the group, awarding her with a plaque of appreciation, thanking her for her help training his troops. She was surprised and proud of course, but the enormity of what just occurred didn't really sink in until a few American contractors who had been in Kuwait for quite a while pulled her aside and said, "Tulsi, that was a *really* big deal. What just hap-pened there has never been done before."

I'm glad these contractors were there to point out the rare na-ture of this event and I'm especially glad that the congresswoman allowed me to retell this story here. It carries a strong message about this important rule. The lesson from my perspective is that even when you are doing something that seems totally natural and normal to you but is considered special to someone else, it's worth taking a second to process the fact that you really made a difference. When others make a point of saying thank you, let their gratitude sink in. It keeps us in touch with just how much our actions have an effect on others.

Representative McSally's moment happened after a very long

and protracted battle to right a wrong, but it also took her a bit by surprise. The events in the story she told me began in 1995. It was when she was deployed to Kuwait that she first discovered female troops deployed next door in Saudi Arabia could not travel off base, even on official business, without wearing the customary head-to-toe gown, called an abaya, and its matching head scarf. Female troops were also not permitted to drive. They had to ride in the back seat of whatever vehicle they were in and they had to be escorted by a male soldier or officer at all times. According to the congresswoman, the troops were also directed to claim the servicewoman as the wife of the male soldier if stopped by the local "religious police," in order to comply with sharia law. Discovering these rules absolutely enraged her. As she put it, "The military was essentially applying the seventh century norms of Saudi Arabia to our troops. It abandoned the American values that we all raised our right hand to die for."

She proceeded to contest these rules for six and a half years. She quietly and diligently worked within the system to get them changed. There were times when the prospect looked bleak. There were times when she was operating under the threat of court martial. And there was the time when her orders took her to Saudi Arabia where she actually had to comply with these demeaning rules. To remedy the situation, she finally filed a lawsuit against Donald Rumsfeld, the defense secretary at the time. She wasn't suing for money, but only to rescind these directives that degraded good order, discipline, and military effectiveness. Ultimately, she worked with members of the House and the Senate to overturn these denigrating policies. It was a great consolation to her when the legislation passed unanimously. The day President Bush signed the law into effect, she watched it on C-SPAN while deployed back in Saudi Arabia. Given the time difference, everyone around her was wondering why she was up in the middle of the night watching this. All she could say to her male peers was, "You don't understand what just happened. It's huge." She didn't say much more to them on the subject because as she explained, "The last thing you want to do is make a big deal about being a woman when you are in the military. As an officer, you need to shut up and follow orders when they are lawful, and you need to speak out when they're not."

But that wasn't the only time she got to *own* her moment for the role she played in getting this policy changed. In 2003, roughly a year after the legislative victory, she was again deployed to Saudi Arabia. It was during the preparations for the Iraq war, and she recalled arriving on a C17 in the dead of night. "I was in-processed by a young enlisted woman, on the hood of a jeep with only a flashlight to help us see what we were signing," she told me. "This enlisted woman handed me my room key, reviewed a copy of my orders, and then gave me a piece of paper saying, 'Now here's this legislation that says you don't have to wear an abaya when you go off base.' She had no idea who I was—but in my heart I was shouting, *I wrote this legislation!*" Congresswoman McSally added that what made the moment even more exciting was that she had insisted the bill include language mandating all female troops be given a written copy of the legislation within forty-eight hours of entering the theater, and the military was clearly complying. She said, "I remember just owning that moment . . . just looking up to the heavens thinking, *Thank God it's over. We finally won. This wrong has been righted, and I'm proud that I made it happen.*"

What I took away from this event was that when you've faced a challenge, applied patience, or persevered and there is no one else around to applaud those efforts, appreciating them yourself is also in order. Taking that moment, even in private, shifts the focus from how daunting the task was to how rewarding it is in the end . . . which is something you will need to remember the next time you step up.

When the Work Is Its Own Reward

Unfortunately, there may be times when your hard work does not get rewarded in the way you hoped it would. Those are times when for your own sake and the sake of others you just have to keep on doing what you are doing.

Military spouse Paola Harrell told me about a three-star general who partnered with a four-star general to form quite a powerful team throughout much of their careers. They really were a dynamic duo. She says the three-star general should have been a four-star general by the time Desert Storm broke out, but the approval process often takes a very long time. That's just the way it is. Nevertheless, the three-star general continued to be the committed leader he had always been. He went into the war with his teammate and throughout it all he showed the commitment of a leader with a whole constellation of stars behind him. When he retired a big party was thrown for him and everyone came. He really owned that moment. He stood tall and worked the room as if he really did have a fourth star. He remained humbled to serve. He did not wear his rank, because you just don't do that. But everything about the way he carried himself told you that he was of the highest caliber. I would say from Paola's description that this general is an example of somebody who had unleashed the power of integrity *and* owned his moment!

I hope that all of these shared experiences will help prepare you for those times when you will face a crowd and need to model the many attributes that got you to your place of honor. With so many examples of bad behavior around us these days, we need reminders of the real qualities that power success.

YOU DESERVE A MEDAL TOO

Have you ever owned a moment? I mean really owned it in some of the ways I've described above? We each have a history filled with opportunities to have been a role model for others. Take a moment to really reflect on the achievements you are most proud of in your lifetime so far. Even if these accomplishments did not come with some kind of public award, celebrate them by yourself or remember them with those who are closest to you, especially if those others were instrumental in helping you arrive at your success. This is a form of owning your moment, even if it is after the fact or done in private. It will remind you of how good it feels to excel and will also inspire you to create other such moments for yourself in the future.

Just as important, ask yourself if you have ever missed an opportunity to own your moment. Was there a time when you could have or should have owned it better? How would you do it now that you're older and wiser? Perfecting the art takes time and some consideration, but it is well worth the effort because it can potentially impact a lot of lives.

While many successful people find that the real reward comes when you are engaged in doing something you love more than when you receive accolades for it, dreaming of getting top honors can still be a powerful motivation for us all. You can be humble and still use these existing benchmarks to set important goals for yourself. What are some of the awards or honors that indicate that kind of progress? Even if they typically take extraordinary efforts or a lifetime to achieve, make a list of them for inspiration. For instance, if you are a student, are you hoping to make the honor roll, achieve cum laude, summa cum laude, or magna cum laude, or graduate with distinction in your field of study? Do you wish to become a Rhodes scholar? If you are an athlete, do you wish to be named MVP of your high school, college, or professional team? Do you wish to win the Heisman Trophy someday? Or an Olympic gold medal? Is attaining a black belt in your preferred martial art something you are interested in instead? You get the idea.

Of course, I realize that not everyone lands these coveted top honors, but aiming for them still has the potential to build greatness in us. Each milestone we reach along the way to the goal instills important lessons and transforms us into more confident and capable people. What are the top honors you are reaching for? Keep your written list in a place where you will be certain to see it from time to time. Having reminders of your goals in plain sight is always helpful.

Also be sure to plot out all the benchmarks you will need to meet along the way to finally reach those highest honors. There are countless other kinds of awards between where you are now and being at the pinnacle of your career that will raise your profile, advance your goals, *and* also inspire others in the process. List those awards as well and work toward them individually. Achieving them one by one may very well help you accomplish your ultimate goals such as those listed above. Then imagine your acceptance speech in front of a mirror or when you are taking a shower. What will you tell others striving to reach the same heights? Giving that speech won't be difficult at all when the time comes, because you will have visualized the moment and the generous ways you are going to share what you've learned.

Remember: You don't have to wait for an honor to be bestowed on you to own your moment; you can create your own opportunities to shine too. Create a space to spotlight and share your knowledge about your work or a special hobby with others who aspire to be as good in that area as you are. Start a blog, vlog, or a YouTube channel. Those who give TED talks, for example, are not only owning their moment, they are grooming others to have a moment someday too.

If you are someone who has already achieved your goals, bear in mind that leadership is not a destination, as I said earlier. Climb higher; create a new level; refuse to allow any kind of ceiling to be placed over your head . . . Or feel free to branch out to a new or related field where your experience and different perspective can make a difference.

Ask yourself: *What other endeavors could my skills be applied to successfully?* Remember, you can own as many moments as your imagination and your efforts allow.

To help develop one of the best attributes a leader can possess, list all the possible times when you could yield the floor more often to others, especially if you have a tendency to monopolize conversations. What can you do better in meetings, in the classroom, in conversations with friends, or even at the family dinner table that would make you a better listener and overall communicator?

As you can see, all this advice doesn't just apply to your career.

While it's true no one gives medals for best spouse, best parent, or best neighbor, there are things these loving people do to celebrate you every day. Noticing these deeds, large and small, for the rewards that they really are is important. How you give and receive gratitude to the people you love sets the tone for how they will own the big and little moments in their lives too. I can think of no better application for this rule.

By the way, I recognize that just by reading this book you are taking steps toward meeting your goals and owning your future moments and I gratefully applaud your efforts. Go conquer the world and share the experience with others along the way.

Rule #9

WHEN THINGS FALL APART, BELIEVE
YOU HAVE THE ANSWER

If you've spent any amount of time in armed conflict or war, then you are intimate with a whole range of feelings from disappointment, frustration, and anger to profound sadness. To survive requires a certain kind of emotional resilience that is built up with experience. My father told me about a situation he endured in Vietnam that would have tested anyone's strength.

He was called one day to go on an urgent mission. He was needed to pick up injured American soldiers and two allies, who if memory serves him correctly, were Australian troops. He immediately headed north to the spot somewhere between Nha Trung and the DMZ. When he arrived, he got out of the helicopter and realized that enemy combatants were also there for pickup. The thought of taking wounded soldiers and the guys they knew had just killed some of their own on the same aircraft together seemed like a form of torture that he wanted no part of. He knew he couldn't do it. He had heard of other pilots who faced the same dilemma and had no choice, but he was determined to keep them separate. While medics worked on the wounded, he stayed on the ground with the combatants until a second helicopter showed. He boarded the combatants on that other aircraft and sped off as fast as he could to get our own men the additional attention they needed. He told me that there were times when being in a situation like that was so traumatic for the soldiers being picked up that they had to go to the hospital to be treated for trauma more than for their physical wounds. He didn't want that to happen to these men so he had to think quickly about how to work effectively around the challenge.

What contributes to emotional resilience is the ability to problem-solve—to find a way to lessen the pain, frustration, anger, or whatever else the experience brings up for you in that moment.

My father had also endured loss. He had survived people who were more than buddies—they were friends and brothers. He has said, "The prospect of losing such a fellow in arms is terrorizing, but the reality is worse." In the thick of action all you can do is try to get a downed soldier to safety. If they don't make it, you still need to keep your head in the fight. Only when you return and the adrenaline has subsided can you begin to deal with the complex and mixed emotions that follow. You are angry at the enemy, gutted by your loss, yet you're also relieved that you made it out alive. My father told me, "As an officer you live every loss along with those you lead. If a fallen soldier was a best friend to one of your men, then he was a best friend to you too." He explained that you have to find ways to memorialize the fallen right away. A talk that honors their life is sometimes all you can do. But you have to really speak to who that person was. Everyone wants to know they will be remembered too should it happen to them. You have to also stress the importance of moving on and getting the job done or you will be mourning more people in the end. Of course, you don't say that, but that is the underlying message.

I hadn't heard him speak of those events until very recently. I was sheltered from some of the realities of war. That is just not the thing you tell a young girl unless you want to worry her more about your safety.

But I was raised with a strong sense that if there is a situation that seems insurmountable to you right now, trust that there are many ways to look for and find the solutions, the words, and the reliable emotions that will help you make sense of it or at least help you cope with it.

STRONG IN THE BROKEN PLACES

My hope is that you never have to experience the pains of war, but contending with a wide range of deep emotions is an inevitable aspect of life in and out of the military. You will have some experiences that really challenge you, even if you employ all nine of my rules. There will definitely be times on your quest for success when these rules will serve as your compass, guiding you safely to higher ground. But there will also be times when you will feel very vulnerable. There may be occasions when you take some incoming fire, too. I don't know a single person with a true fighting spirit who hasn't had to face a trying situation head-on at some point in their journey.

It's during these challenging times that my final rule, "When Things Fall Apart, Believe You Have the Answer," will prove to you and everyone else that you can be tougher than military-grade steel if you have to be. This rule has the potential to be your best protection against defeat. It demands that you trust yourself in the most difficult of circumstances. It reminds you that because of all of your training—all of the developmental work you have been doing on yourself—you will come to a better understanding of the situation and your ability to weather it. Developing emotional resilience and leaning on it when times get tough is essential. Sometimes emotional resilience is a matter of temperament, but it is also a learned and practiced art.

LEARNING BY HEART

The value of this rule became clearer and clearer to me over time. As I said, emotional resilience is something that builds over many experiences. What seemed to be an ordeal when I was much younger paled in comparison to challenges later in life and certainly to the challenges my dad faced in war.

One of my earliest memories of moving quickly to address disappointment before it could stall my progress occurred during the year I was applying to colleges. In the hearts and minds of most teenagers, that's a pretty rough time. There is a lot of pressure not just to be your best self, but to make sure all the schools you are applying to see that version of you too. Despite how intimidating the process can be, I was excited and curious to see what my future would hold.

My father had just retired from the military and he and my mom had decided to settle in California, so we headed there together to check out schools that might be a good match for my interests. I loved the East Coast, but I was clearly attracted by the West Coast weather. I had set my heart on UC Davis, Santa Cruz, or Santa Barbara, though I applied to a few other schools as well. I did my homework regarding their curriculums, their faculty, and the breadth of their extracurricular activities, thoroughly weighing the pros and cons of each school. The good news was that all of them had excellent communications programs. I wasn't sure if I wanted to write or produce yet, so having general communications skills—script or screenwriting experience—was important to me.

Once I completed my applications I was naturally anxious for the schools' replies. I talked with my parents, as all kids do, about the impatience I was feeling. I'm not sure how the subject came up, but they were surprised to learn that I had not listed my ethnicity on the paperwork. All my friends were shocked too that I didn't apply as a minority candidate. When I didn't get into UC Davis I was disappointed. Although I was a good student and had very respectable SAT scores, I knew from the start that Davis was a highly competitive university. They received so many applicants each year that I suspected I might not get in. But I was still upset to receive the bad news. I wondered if not checking that box hurt my chances. I also began wondering what more I could do to sway the other schools' decisions. My concerns engendered an interesting talk around the dinner table one night. I questioned aloud how not making a distinction about race could affect my prospects of getting into some of the other universities. When my dad asked why I didn't identify myself as a minority candidate in the first place, I simply said, "I just don't see myself that way." My father's response was very specific. I recall it almost verbatim. "If you don't see yourself that way, it's okay. Other people see you that way, so if you are concerned about not getting into the other schools, what you need to do is write a letter to those schools telling them all the reasons why you would be an asset. Make the best case for yourself that you can. Since you didn't check the African American box before, you're *not* going to check it in that letter either. You're going to find a way to convince the admissions committee that you're a great candidate no matter what." And that is exactly what I did.

As I look back on that experience now, I realize it was a similar logic that led my dad to join the Army. In the military you are free to be yourself and to progress because of the abilities you bring to each position you seek. You can be whoever you want to be so long as you are consistently you, possess the right skills, and sell the fact that you have those skills. As you are going through the ranks of the military, you're green above all else. You're not brown; you're not white. You are simply you. Your abilities are what carry you forward. Think about it: When troops walk around in camouflage, how can you tell a colonel from a lieutenant or a sergeant from a general? You tell it by their behavior and their ability to assert themselves and their leadership qualities. *That's how.*

My father understood how disheartening it was to me that the color of my skin might have anything to do with my getting into school. In encouraging me to write those follow-up letters his message couldn't be clearer: Show them your best self and let the integrity of that choice drive you to succeed on this mission and any other one you pursue in your future. Tucked into that lesson was one on *emotional resilience* too. When you hit a bump in the road you've got to figure out the best way to keep it from stopping your forward motion. In this case, that bump was disappointment that the question of race mattered at all, and concern that I might not get into a school if I didn't do everything I could to persuade the decision-makers. That's a heck of a lesson for a seventeen-year-old to learn.

By the way, I acted on my dad's wisdom and wrote that letter. I was accepted to several schools after that, including UC Santa Barbara, which is where I happily spent the next four years of my life. During this process I also figured out that if you can just reach up and easily grab something, it probably doesn't have a lot of value. Your effort has to match your purpose, your mission, and that all-important goal.

There were other times in my life, as you now know, when I acquired additional layers of emotional resilience. Reaching a career impasse that warranted me innovating around the obstacle—as I did when I developed my radio show—was one such example. Finding the resolve to stop my stalker, hold him accountable for his actions, and prevent him from doing harm to me or anyone else in the future was certainly another example. But as challenging as these experiences were, none of them were as devastating as the one that truly defined this rule.

Because this chapter is not just about the times when the roof leaks; it's about the times when things *really* fall apart—when the whole house comes crashing down—allow me to tell you about a particularly overwhelming time in my life when even my father, who has dealt with so much in his days, was acquiring a new layer of emotional resilience along with me.

THE MOURNING AFTER

The date was November 21, 2016. To say that was a day when everything crumbled for me is an understatement. It was the day of my mother's passing. Her death was so unexpected; it left my heart severed more than broken.

I now know why people use these kinds of words to describe losing somebody they love so much. Because there are so many touchstones in your existence that connect to your parents, losing a mother or a father could break your heart over and over again. Something as simple as a smell in the kitchen could do it. Or I'd be at a perfume counter weeks later when another scent I associated with my mother would trigger my deepest darkest hurts. Love sneaks up on you. It envelops you, so when someone who expresses it so freely and so often departs and you no longer hear her voice, there is a void in your life that nothing else can fill.

But despite these shared expressions and experiences of hurt and pain, what nobody ever talks about is how to actually mend your heart after loss. Time may heal it. I know that's what people say, but it hasn't for me, and it doesn't for many other people, whether or not they were as close with their parents as I've been with mine.

Somehow, despite the depth of our losses, we still have to find and exercise the emotional resilience within us to continue living our life—the life we were put on this earth to lead until our own demise. We can't just quit living while we are alive because someone we love is dying on us, or has died. I don't know how other people do that, but in my case, I watched my parents' valiant efforts to sort it out as it was happening, and tried to do the same.

Yes, my father had experience with grief in the war and was certainly conditioned by that experience to press on after loss as a matter of survival, but this was a heartache of a whole different magnitude. This was his *wife*, his life partner. There had been no precedent for this depth of sorrow.

Beginning on September 15, 2016, when I received that fateful call from him telling me that he had just called 911 because my mother had collapsed, I saw this man push past his own confusion and fear and immediately kick into action. My mom had told him that she was bleeding, but my dad didn't see any blood. Noticing how quickly she was fading, he assumed the bleeding was internal. In addition to calling an ambulance he had the presence of mind to call my aunt Vanessa, who is a nurse. She assured him that she would meet him at the hospital and would know what to do. My father then called me. He sensed time was fleeting and he wanted me to know what was happening. I asked him to put the phone to my mother's ear. I told her that I loved her and then asked if she could talk. Her response was so weak I don't know why I did that. I should have known that if there was any breath left in her she would spend it on me. She told me she never really thought it would feel like this. She didn't want to breathe anymore. She was so tired. Seconds later there was pounding at the door and the emergency medical team took over. But before they did, she said that she had been taking some medication and she wasn't sure if that was the problem. Until then, I had been completely unaware that she was ill.

Things were moving at a frenetic pace. My father took back the phone and told me to reach out to my aunts and uncles.

"I love you," he said. "I'm sorry this is happening."

And then he hung up. I don't know how he got out most of that information because, as it turns out, my mother was very close to death at that point and he knew it.

I was in New York and they were in Dallas but I followed my dad's orders. When I couldn't get through to my sister, I texted her. I then called my father's younger brothers Tim and Ronnie.

The rest of my family is spread out in Dallas Metro and while they all offered for me to stay with them, I wanted to be in a hotel close to the hospital. My father never left my mother's bedside so he didn't need a place, but my relatives helped locate one for me. That emergency call from my dad came on a Thursday. I caught the earliest plane I could, but with flight delays, I didn't get there until the next afternoon.

When I walked in the room, my mother had just awakened. She was very glad to see me. The doctors had given her a lot of blood and she was starting to come around. They had also begun to give my father some further information about her condition. He didn't immediately share it, which frustrated my sister Annissa and me. Neither of my parents told us much about their health in later life as you will recall from the story about my father's earlier close brush with death. But because I have my own children, I understand that if you give loved ones too much information it disturbs their lives. In my end of days, if I should ever get the heads-up by even a few weeks the way my mom did, I probably will be close to the vest with what I know too. I'll keep it to myself until I can no longer be the one disseminating that news—until it's the doctors telling everybody what they need to know. When you love somebody and you understand the end is near, there's no need to disrupt the rhythm and flow of things for them—especially if you helped to create those loved ones. They're my legacy. Instead, I'm going to fill them up with what I know will help them rebound, and that's what my mother did for me.

I stayed with my mom until Saturday night when I had to fly back home to do my Sunday night show. Then on Friday, after the last *Outnumbered* of the week, I hopped on a plane to Dallas again, arriving in time for dinner. I shuttled back and forth like this for three weeks. By the end of that third week, I found out that my mother had stage four lung cancer. She hadn't divulged that information to anyone earlier because her sister Mary, whom she was very close to, had been battling stage four breast cancer at the same time and lost her life to it earlier that month. My aunt's funeral was Friday, September 2. The last picture I have of my mom standing was in her living room as she was hosting what we call "the afterglow"—the reception following my aunt Mary's funeral. Twelve days later, my mother was admitted to the hospital facing the same fate.

She had a tumor resting on her lung and some sort of mass near her kidney that they couldn't get to. The biopsy almost killed her. She didn't wake up for a week after that. It's a simple procedure for most people but her breathing was so labored because of that tumor, it took every ounce of energy from her. It was decided that she would undergo radiation, but surgery was out of the question. She could never withstand it. The radiation shrank the tumor a little bit, but she still needed a tracheotomy to help her breathe. She was fading away in front of our eyes. It was happening all too quickly for me. I felt like everything was just flashing by, like when you stick your head out of a car window while the car is moving—you know, how a dog does—and you can barely catch your breath. For some reason, dogs don't mind that, but I did. I needed the fresh air to revive me but the car I was in was going one hundred miles per hour toward a destination I didn't know.

When I was back in New York, I'd call my mother several times a day. I would just ask my dad to put the phone up next to her so I could tell her how much I loved her. She must have heard the words "I love you" more times during those few weeks than she did her entire life. We had been phone buddies ever since I went to college. She was the person I turned to regularly. The one who helped me navigate my incredibly full schedule as I got more successful—the one I always told the good news, the bad news, and the "news" news to. I mean, some of the things I'd say on TV were thoughts I'd run past her first—especially if there was something the magnitude of a Ferguson, Missouri, happening.

I definitely thought of her after Charlottesville, Virginia. It seems as if a lot of the bigger news events of the past few years had taken us backward in time to decades before I was alive. Heck, we were having the kinds of conversations about race in America after the news about Trayvon Martin broke that we hadn't had in this country since the 1940s. People were talking about it on TV, in their homes, at the gas station, and everywhere else. President Obama said, "Trayvon Martin could have been me thirty-five years ago."

I remember some of my mom's white friends were upset. They felt as if the whole world was comparing them to what they called "the kinds of white people who just don't care." Of course, the irony, as my mom and I discussed, is that the man who shot and killed Trayvon Martin and was acquitted of second-degree murder was part Hispanic. George Zimmerman's mother was reportedly from Peru originally and is believed to have some African lineage, so he might have understood more about the idiosyncrasies of being a minority than anyone ever considered. I brought this up on the air with a couple of guests. One was George Zimmerman's brother; the other was Reverend Jesse Jackson. It was amid the national protests and dialogue surrounding the case. I observed that the biggest issue was how people were talking past one another. They were not seeing each other as individuals.

My mom had a way of breaking things down. She didn't even know what a producer does, and she certainly was not a content driver anywhere. Nevertheless, she was great at prompting me to see every single person for who they are individually, coming into an event. She always reminded me to make who they are matter, not just because of what they did at the event, but because of her belief that they were there for a reason. She would say, "If God wanted you to be someplace else, He'd put you there." She felt that way about everybody, even people making horrendous mistakes. Now follow her thinking on this with me: "Yes, we have free choice according to the Bible," she'd say. "But in a split second, God can move you if He so chooses. You may have willed yourself to be in that spot, but more likely something pulled you there—some point of destiny got you there. *So what lesson were you put there to learn?* The mistake most people make is that they see themselves as the higher power in those moments when the big decisions are to be made. Instead of letting the Divine guide their next step, they act on their own rash instincts."

She'd tell me again and again that I always have the ability to pray and listen for the answers in a calm and still position—that there are always answers that will come to you at those critical moments. She also reminded me of a line I say all the time on television, "You play like you practice." So in those split-seconds when you react impulsively—when you might be tempted to pick up a gun—if you have practiced greater control and awareness and have a connection with the Lord, what will likely come quickly to your mind is a more peaceable way to respond. She would say, "You only need to practice one thing all the other times of your life, and that is to be pure of heart, so that when life calls on you to learn a lesson, when life puts you in a position to make a difficult decision, the one you make will be one you can live with because it comes from a good place."

My mom was the queen of my inner circle. I loved those conversations with her and I was already beginning to miss them. Saying, "I love you" over and over again was the deepest expression of my gratitude for those talks when they could no longer be had.

On Thursday, November 10, when I returned to Dallas again, my dad was a soldier with a battle plan. He was determined to find a hospice facility. We had all made the decision together a few days earlier. My mother had been part of that process as much as she could be. So my sister and I were deployed to find just the right one from a list of several places. When Mom was sedated, we scooped Dad up to show him the final selections. He liked one place more than the others and said that he wanted her moved there the very next day. I couldn't quite figure out the timing of it all. It seemed rushed. But I assumed it was a military thing—once a soldier comes up with a solid plan he wastes no time executing it.

The next morning, before moving Mom into hospice, I was reading Scriptures to her. The TV was playing softly in the background. My show *Outnumbered* was on. She saw somebody else in my seat but she didn't have the little piece you insert in your trach tube to help you talk, so she pointed and mouthed, "Why are you here?" When I told her I wanted to spend time with her, her lips moved again, "I'm not dead yet," she replied. Then she reached around and finally found that missing piece and said, "My journey is not your journey. Trust me, when your time comes it will be hell too. Wait your turn." God, I can barely repeat those words. "Wait your turn," she said to me. "I built you to take it. You'll say goodbye. You'll be fine," she continued. "I'll still be with you if you let me. You have what it takes when this falls apart. You do. I have to make sure you believe that."

Those words were more than she had said in all the combined weeks she spent in the hospital. And boy did I feel their intensity. Then she began to cough. That cough racked her body from head to toe. It hurt her so bad that it hurt me. I ran to get a nurse, but when I reached the hallway it was as if all the lights went out. I was crashing. With very heavy steps, I made it to the nurses' station. By then, they were already mobilized to get to her room because they heard that awful cough too. They told me to stay out and I did. My dad and my uncles Tim and Ronnie had gone down to the break room for just a second. My father never left the hospital so they were trying to convince him to go home to rest and take a shower, but the best they could do was to get him to walk around a little bit. The nurses got Mom stabilized before they returned and told me that she needed to sleep. I just stayed in the room holding her hand as she dozed off. Every now and then she would open her eyes and smile the most heart-permeating, proud-mom smile you could imagine.

The next morning we were moving her according to Dad's plan. As the ambulance took my mom from the hospital she had been in for several weeks to another hospital-like setting where we knew she'd never leave, I noticed that there were flags waving in the breeze out front. It was odd that I hadn't seen them the day before. I have to say that when someone you love is about to pass away, your concentration tends to be totally focused on that person, but I still didn't understand how I could have missed that detail earlier. And then it occurred to me. You know why she had to move into the facility on that day? *Because it was Veteran's Day!* November 11, 2016. That Friday, Dad wanted her on her way for a reason. My parents were like two warriors in a bunker planning every move. Although Mom was sedated throughout the day, she apparently had some clarity at night, and that's when they'd talk. They had chosen this facility because it was the only one that would allow Dad to stay with her, and they had chosen this move date for what were now obvious motives.

Her suite at the hospice was beautiful. It was like a small apartment, but without a kitchen. What it had instead was an awesome veranda and a set of gorgeous French double doors that led to a courtyard. My dad wheeled my mom out there to sit in the sun. The place was big enough for our family members—my eleven cousins and my aunts and uncles who lived in the Dallas metro area—to come and visit. My aunts are truly amazing. They all arrived with flowers and food. Aunt Vanessa, who is my uncle Tim's wife and also the person who guided my dad through those harrowing moments after calling 911, was there. My mom's sisters Aunt Maxine and Aunt Ruby were too. They are such funny women. They fight all the time but they can't live without each other. We already missed the presence of my aunt Mary. Her nickname was Pig because she squealed with laughter at everything—I really longed for her joy that day. I sure could have used it. But my dad was a true soldier. He was determined to keep us positive and focused on the mission. He told us that it was important to live in the moment and to fulfill any desire that Mom had. She liked ice cream, but as a diabetic the nurses at the hospital wouldn't let her have it. Here the rules were different so we let her know that she could eat it to her heart's content, and we made plenty of it available to her, though by that time, she had no appetite and could barely tolerate water.

After that day, I had to make one more trip back to New York.

In the time I spent so far saying goodbye to my mother, I had realized how unsustainable a six-day workweek was. I had asked for some time off from the Sunday night show right after the day I discovered it was stage four cancer we were dealing with, but I knew some additional choices in my life still needed to be revisited. I was really grateful to work at a place that valued me and was so considerate of the journey I was currently on. I was also very moved by all the flowers, notes, e-mails, and text messages my coworkers sent. They were, each and every one of them, a blessing.

But what my mom was helping me to discover there in Dallas is that we have more time than we think *and* we have less time too. We have more time to complain and do things like shop because they take less energy. But we also have less time to love and to be engaged in relationships of all kinds with others because those are major commitments. When you grumble about stuff or go for a little retail therapy, it doesn't require a lot of brainpower. It doesn't consume a lot of energy. It doesn't take much creativity either. But when you're raising a family and you need to be at a gymnastic meet or you need to be at a soccer game or you need to just give the other parent a break because they've earned it too—when you need to be present in your marriage, in your interactions as a daughter, sister, and friend—that level of energy is different. It's electric. It's life-burning energy. You can't just give that away. It is intended to be spent on those who matter and those who will appreciate it the most. I love what I do and am grateful that everybody in my family gave me a pass for three years to be gone every Sunday through Friday—and sometimes Saturday too if news broke on that seventh day as well. But I owed it to the family that I love so much to restore some greater balance—to allocate energies differently. I was going to work for another week before returning to Dallas for us all to spend Thanksgiving together. After that, I would come up with a plan.

Before I left, though, I caught sight of a notebook by my mother's bedside. It contained the rest of my father's plan. He called it a "going home plan." It was filled with notes about a military spouse burial to be held after my mother's funeral. He was talking to people at Arlington Cemetery—a vast military memorial park in Arlington, Texas. It made perfect sense. The military had always grounded our family. We always relied on our military principles. Of course, the military would be behind us as we faced our greatest headwind—the hardship of life leaving us.

While it gave me comfort to know that my dad was leaning in for support from his A-team—the Army—something about that notebook nagged at my heart. To this day, I'm not sure what it was, but I believe in God so I suspect it was His Divine Grace at work. Tony, the girls, and I were scheduled to arrive back in Dallas on a Wednesday but because of that nagging feeling, I changed our tickets and flew back on Monday, November 21, instead. My mother passed just three hours after my plane landed. I was able to see her and be with her right up until midnight when the undertaker came to pick up her body. I would not have been there if I didn't have that tug on my heartstrings.

From that point forward, my father, sister, and I shifted into high gear. We were unstoppable forces. The pastor at the funeral home said he never saw anybody plan something so big so fast in his whole career and that man was just over seventy years of age, I'm certain. The funeral was a funeral. It was sad, although we did sing a rousing rendition of "This Little Light of Mine" that I led. I didn't know that I remembered the words until I started singing spontaneously at the end of the eulogy I had given. We all had big smiles on our faces because my mother loved gospel and she loved that song, though we sing it a little bit differently. It's got some backbone to it when we do it. By the time of the second service—the spousal burial held at the top of a very tall hillside at the center of the cemetery—there was a gentle wind blowing even though there was still warmth to the Texas air. The skies had opened up and delivered a severe thunderstorm hours before we were set to lay Mom to rest there. Just the closest of family were present at this ceremony led by a military veteran who introduced my father to give my mother his final salute. My dad stood at my mother's casket and that's when we heard these words for the first time, "I have led so many into battle. I have hoped to return so many times, and in each moment, I knew that I had the greatest soldier I have ever known on my side. I salute you, Shirley Temple Harris. I will love you forever."

There are two things I have come to know for sure after this journey. The first is that my father and mother were each other's most trusted special forces. My father reminded us of that when he made certain that my mother began her journey to the other side in hospice care on Veteran's Day and concluded it with this military spouse burial in a most sacred and amazing place they chose together. My sister and I may not have been privy to their late-night conversations at the time this was all thought out, but the essence of those conversations was being revealed now. My parents had not just prepared a funeral; they had prepared a message. It was one of love, but it had a tone of discipline to it. They saw our last weeks together as an opportunity to gain a renewed spirit and understanding about how precious life is. They wanted the experience to change us because it was one worth changing for. They wanted us to know that we only grow in one direction. No one gets to go backward. Learning to *bounce forward* is critical. They wanted us to understand that the same values that carry us through this world will carry us into the next. My mother would be okay in that world and we would eventually be okay in this one. While things most definitely fell apart for me during that difficult time, therein was the answer as to how to move on. How to be resilient. How to survive.

Some weeks later I decided that I would try to talk about the experience. I wanted to find some meaningful channel for my grief, for my own sake and the sake of anyone else who has ever felt so bereft. I was scheduled to give a speech so I broached the subject then. I told the members of the audience gathered there:

> When things fall apart we really do have the mechanisms—the resilience—to "bounce forward." I've always disliked the phrase "bounce back." I mean really, who wants to go backward? Things are never going to be the same. Whatever it was that got you to this point is still going to happen, but now you'll have the forecast of it happening, which could technically make it more difficult to overcome and survive because, of course, you can't change the past. I guess you could only relive it. But who would want to do that? Even when times in the past were glorious, they still led to this point right here. The time in between isn't any longer, any richer, any deeper. Knowing that the end is coming might make it worse, so the goal is always to bounce forward.

The speech helped because what I realized in writing it was that this sentiment really wasn't mine alone. My parents had put those thoughts in my mind and heart during my time of shock and sadness when they became actual examples of bouncing forward themselves.

Sometime in the future, or maybe even right now, you may feel your world crumbling too. Perhaps that's why you gravitated to this book. It may be due to the loss of a job. It may be because you or someone you love is also waging war against a disease. You may be picking up the pieces of your home after a natural disaster. You may be involved in a divorce. Or maybe you're the person in a marriage who really doesn't want to give up. Whatever it is, if it feels like everything is falling apart, please heed the message of my mother's last days and believe that you really do have the answers. My greatest lesson about overcoming hardship did not come from a famous general or battle, but rather from the end to her journey. This wise woman, who lived most of her adult life in that rare space between the military and civilian worlds, had a clear enough perspective to see that whenever you are grappling with loss and it feels as if the fire has left you, that is the time to remember what you were fighting for to begin with: Life. Reclaim it. Rethink it. Rebuild it. Make it the best life it can be no matter what the circumstances. We only grow in one direction. No one gets to go backward. The part about *bouncing forward* is critical.

BUILDING YOUR EMOTIONAL FOUNDATION

As it turns out, I wrote this chapter on the one-year anniversary of my mother's passing, so I am still learning ways to bounce forward. Collecting wisdom from my early life with her and my father for this book is just one of those ways. Recalling now how she told me that she built me to be able to withstand her death, I know that what she meant is she and my father tried to teach me lessons that would make me emotionally resilient. So those are the types of exercises we will focus on here. With a stronger emotional foundation, the hope is that we will all be better able to move forward meaningfully when things fall apart.

As I said earlier, disappointment and grief is sure to visit us all. At some point each of us will lose the personal rock we leaned on most. We are lucky to have had them in our lives, but the strength we cultivate *before* as well as after our loss is what will make all the difference in how we ultimately cope.

As always, let's start out with a few questions:

Have you ever faced a difficult challenge and been surprised that you got through it? If so, what inner resources did you rely on? It can be helpful to take inventory of all the strengths you've forgotten about or didn't even realize you have. You may not consider yourself the most organized person, for instance, but if that skill kicked in and played a part in powering you through your prior difficult situation, then you know that ability is available to you, but it has to be developed further.

Some experts say that to build any kind of resilience you should take on new challenges that enable you to grow in those areas where growth is needed most. It's good to try new things that require you to invest more of your emotional, mental, and/ or physical self. Doing so helps you stretch beyond your present capacity. It is also better to acquire the skills that contribute to mental and emotional strength in a situation of your choosing than in a crisis situation. Once that strength takes hold it will be there for you when you need it again. For example, as a journalist anchoring my first newscasts in Greenville, North Carolina, I would challenge myself to be as familiar as possible with the teleprompter copy before a show. TV journalists usually review copy in advance, but I went beyond that reviewing process so I would anchor much more of the show without a teleprompter. It was terrifying to go without that safety net. I was already nervous enough just being on camera! But it was worth working through that fear. To this day some of my mentors, who are now my peers at the network level, praise me for being a strong ad-libber. My ability to extemporize derives from learning very early on not to depend on what is in front of me even if it was already carefully written and prepared. The teleprompter copy provides a little backup for me, but I don't rely on it completely. I have the ability to know a story well enough to tell it without that help, which means when breaking news happens it's natural for me to ad-lib.

If you are in a challenging situation right now, can you name the emotions you are feeling? Are any of them fear or worry? If so, bear in mind that in this instance they may be your enemy because they have the potential to keep you from dealing with your crisis. Once you recognize them as such, there is no way you will join forces with them. And if they can't join forces with you, they can't control you. This is the best of military thinking for sure.

With these distractions out of your way, try to visualize the outcome you are hoping for, no matter how difficult it may seem to achieve. From where you are standing at this moment to the point of attaining your goal, how many steps do you count? What are those steps? How many of them seem doable? Focus on the ones you have identified as possible. This will put energy in motion and move you closer to your goal. Focusing on the positive sets your mind in only one direction at a time—the direction that gets you to your destination. If you are consumed by thoughts of all the things that could go wrong, that is the course your brain will take instead. You don't want to do that. Negative thinking will only get you lost. It serves no purpose on this mission.

Now that you've disengaged the parts of your mind that could get in your way *and* you have actively engaged the parts that are primed for success in facing and overcoming your challenge, you have to call in your special forces. Who has the skills to help you tackle the obstacles you know you can't? Bear in mind that bringing in a support team does not mean you are any less resilient; it just means you are resourceful. Assign everyone his or her role and act in unison.

If your optimism wanes at any point during this process, it helps to remember the others you may be doing this for. I set goals for myself, but I also bear in mind how much of what I do might benefit my family. When my girls get to see their mom persist and live out her dreams, they will believe anything is possible too. Somehow seeing the big picture sends a message to my subconscious: "Dig deep. There are more people than just me counting on you."

When you emerge from the challenge having succeeded, you will have acquired more emotional resilience than you had before. If you were up against ginormous odds and you only got by with better-than-hoped-for results instead of full victory, take heart because you will have gained much from the effort. Many people who have helped loved ones survive cancer for years more, months more, weeks more, or even days more than their prognosis indicated have felt greater peace for the added time they had with each other. The outcome was inevitable but the emotional resilience they maintained helped everyone involved to make the most of those moments together.

While I wish you a life of peace and joy, I hope this advice helps fortify you for the times when things do fall apart.

MISSION DEBRIEFING

Before I send you cadets on your way, armed with my best rules for achieving success in your own lives, let's just review for a few minutes.

We began this book by noting that we are living in a pivotal time in history—our own personal histories as well as the world's. As you arrive at the last page of this book, you will possess newly acquired tools that enable you to be a real change-maker. There will be challenges ahead of you, but if you stay ready, I am confident that you will rise to meet them.

So many of you are already confronting tough issues. Our culture is presently dealing with its own demons because we have collectively demanded it to. Too many of us have found ourselves in the midst of a maelstrom as the extent of the sexual and racial politics in our workplaces and beyond were revealed to us in the last year or so. Some have said at Fox News, we were among the first to have to handle such red-hot allegations, firings, lawsuits, and more. Since then, of course, the problem has proven to be endemic throughout the nation, including other media outlets, Hollywood, and even on Capitol Hill.

We owe a huge debt of gratitude to those fierce female victims—and in more rare instances, the male victims—who spoke out and emboldened so many others to lift their voices. That's thinking like a general!

Women, strengthened by solidarity, are now taking back their power. The #metoo movement helped many reclaim their dignity. More and more, we are also seeing companies act swiftly and responsibly, purging predators from their premises and their payrolls when evidence of their wrongdoing is presented. We've seen Congress legislate changes to protect members of our armed services from sexual harassment and we've seen the military initiate changes in policy of its own accord.

On the day I am penning these closing words to you, we have also seen Congress move to make sexual harassment training mandatory for all its members and to dissolve the secret slush fund that in part used taxpayers' hard-earned dollars to cover up such misdeeds.

If we broadly look at all of this as a chapter in America's story, this is just the kind of moment we can own. After all, we Americans don't cut and run. When things fall apart, we believe we have the answer.

VICTORY IS ON THE HORIZON

Discrimination is not the only demon we will have to face, of course. There will always be people or situations that for a host of reasons test our patience or threaten to distract us from our purpose. In those times, it is especially important that we unleash the power of our integrity. To do that, you must keep your emotions in check. You must look ahead and see all the possibilities. You will get nowhere if you look back and dwell on the hurt or if you allow others' limitations to become yours. Let the American military creed of sticking to your mission when others might cut and run, guide you. Whenever I get flak from other people or I hit some unexpected turbulence—and you know I have—I decide which responses might deter me from my goals and which ones are more likely to push me in the direction of meeting those goals.

In terms my dad might use, "Whenever I feel as if I'm flying against the wind, I choose to soar." I choose to rise above my circumstances—to get out of the line of fire and see things from a different vantage point. When I am placed in a difficult position, I ask myself if it is also a rare position. Is it one where a can-do attitude offers more than hope to people looking for answers to the same dilemma? Is it one where I can possibly model a path forward for those who feel the odds are stacked against them? One where I can inspire some of tomorrow's doers?

No matter what the challenge, there will be times to speak up forcefully; there will be times to take stealth yet decisive action; and there will be times when both approaches apply. Make your best choice and follow through. Recruit your special forces, devise your mission, and proceed with dedication to the overall objective, which is remaining a beacon of light and hope to the world.

Are you catching the rules in play here? This is a time for Americans—you in particular—to use as many of these nine rules as needed to meet the challenges and the opportunities ahead of you. I say go forth and use them all!

ACKNOWLEDGMENTS

Thank you seems too tiny a phrase to capture my total gratitude and indebtedness to the people who invested in turning my most popular motivational speech "9 Rules of Engagement" into a book. So, let me put it this way: From the moment I put pen to paper (yeah, I write old-school), angels began appearing in my life! But for a season, my special forces grew exponentially. Glad to have served with them on this project.

Let me list and heap praise and love on those who helped me glide through this writing project: the wonderful publishing team at HarperCollins especially Lisa Sharkey and Matt Harper; Cait Hoyt at CAA Books for a coffee meeting and long talks that changed the arc of my writing career; Olivia Metzger at OManagement and Ali Spiesman at CAA Talent for their unmatched belief in my ability to see it through, as the news cycle often blinded my way forward; my Fox News Channel *Outnumbered* and *Outnumbered Overtime with Harris Faulkner* teams for giving me support when they didn't even know I needed it; and to others in my professional family at Fox News Channel who value the winding road which always leads to the truth.

A special thanks to the amazing military leaders, past and present, who generously sat with me for interviews. And trust me when I tell you—I asked a lot of questions! Retired four-star General Jack Keane, Congresswoman Tulsi Gabbard (D-HI), Congresswoman Martha McSally (R-AZ), and Paolo Harrell, wife of Major General James Harrell.

And, to Hope Innelli. Thanks for being on my tactical team. Take a bow, grab a Moscow Mule, and let's party!

Hugs and sweet joy to my husband, Tony, and our daughters, Bella and Danika. They helped me gather stories from Grandpa Bobby, or as readers now know him, Lieutenant Colonel Bob Harris.

Gratitude to my sister, Annissa, and my niece, Audrey, for supporting Dad as he recounted decades of American history for this book.

And Dad, we did it . . . with help from Mom in heaven. My civilian salute to you both and all my love.

REFERENCES

RULE #1: RECRUIT YOUR SPECIAL FORCES

B. J. Austin, "Remembering Sam Tasby, Key Figure in Dallas School Desegregation Case," Kera News, last modified August 17, 2015, http://
keranews.org/post/remembering-sam-tasby-key-figure-dallas-school
-desegregation-case.

Southern Methodist University Dedman School of Law, "DISD Desegregation Litigation Archives," http://library.law.smu.edu/Collections/DISD
/Background-Info, accessed December 4, 2017.

RULE #2: DEAL WITH YOUR DEMONS

"Norway Introduces Compulsory Military Service for Women, Bunking
Them in Mixed Dorms with Men," *The Straits Times,* last modified
August 25, 2016, http://www.straitstimes.com/world/europe/norway
-introduces-compulsory-military-service-for-women-bunking-them-in
-mixed-dorms.

Kevin Ponniah, "Meet the Hunter Troop: Norway's Tough-as-Nails Female
Soldiers," BBC News, Elverum, last modified March 31, 2017, http://
www.bbc.com/news/world-europe-39434655.

RULE #3: STAY READY

BTWB Press, "Memorial Day Murph: Who? What? Why?" last modified

May 28, 2013, https://blog.beyondthewhiteboard.com/2016/05/26 /memorial-day-murph-who-what-why/.

Carolyn Gregoire, "Why Silence Is So Good for Your Brain," *The Huffington Post*, last modified January 9, 2017, https://www.huffingtonpost .com/entry/silence-brain-benefits_us_56d83967e4b0000de4037004.

Barbara Bradley Hagerty, "Prayer May Reshape Your Brain . . . and Your Reality," NPR, last modified May 20, 2009, https://www.npr.org/templates /story/story.php?storyId=104310443.

Jon Hamilton, "A Protein That Moves from Muscle to Brain May Tie Exercise to Memory," NPR, last modified June 23, 2016, https://www.npr .org/sections/health-shots/2016/06/23/483245084/a-protein-that -moves-from-muscle-to-brain-may-tie-exercise-to-memory.

Imke Kirste, Zeina Nicola, Golo Kronenberg, Tara Walker, Robert Liu, and Gerd Kempermann, "Is Silence Golden? Effects of Auditory Stimuli and Their Absence on Adult Hippocampal Neurogenesis," *Brain Structure & Function*, (2013), 10.1007/s00429-013-0679–3.

Sarah Knapton, ed., "Exercise Triggers Brain Cell Growth and Improves Memory, Scientists Prove," *The Telegraph*, last modified June 23, 2016, http://www.telegraph.co.uk/science/2016/06/23/exercise-triggers -brain-cell-growth-and-improves-memory-scientists/.

Lt. Michael P. Murphy Memorial Scholarship Foundation, accessed September 13, 2017, https://murphfoundation.org/biography/.

Stew Smith, "Air Force BMT Physical Fitness Test," military.com, accessed September 11, 2017, http://www.military.com/military-fitness/air-force -fitness-requirements/air-force-basic-military-training-fitness-test.

Stew Smith, "Air Force Special Tactics Fitness Training," military.com, accessed November 22, 2017, https://www.military.com/military-fitness /air-force-special-operations/air-force-special-tactics-fitness-training.

Stew Smith, "Train Before You Enter the Military," military.com, accessed

October 22, 2017, https://www.military.com/military-fitness/health
/training-before-you-enter-military#.Wa78oymEe8Q.email.

RULE #7: THINK LIKE A GENERAL

"8 Wonders of People/Buffalo Soldiers, Fort Leavenworth," Kansas Sampler
Foundation, accessed November 28, 2017, https://www.kansassampler
.org/8wonders/peopleresults.php?id=313.

"Fort Leavenworth National Cemetery," U.S. Department of Veterans
Affairs, last modified August 28, 2017, https://www.cem.va.gov/cems
/nchp/ftleavenworth.asp.

"Historic Fort Leavenworth," accessed November 28, 2017, http://www
.kansastravel.org/fortleavenworth.htm.

ABOUT THE AUTHOR

HARRIS FAULKNER anchors her daytime show, *Outnumbered Overtime with Harris Faulkner*, in addition to cohosting the talk show *Outnumbered*. In 2017, she moderated the Women's Inaugural Breakfast, a bipartisan inauguration event in Washington, DC. She lives in New York City.